TO BE A PILGRIM

Basil Hume OSB
Cardinal Archbishop of Westminster

To be a Pilgrim
A Spiritual Notebook

St Paul Publications | **SPCK**

SPCK
Holy Trinity Church
Marylebone Road
London NW1 4DU

British Library Cataloguing in Publication Data

Hume, Basil
   To be a pilgrim
   1. Christian life
   I. Title
   248.4   BV4501.2

ISBN 0-281-04121-0 (hardbound)
ISBN 0-281-04109-1 (paperback)

St Paul Publications
Middlegreen, Slough SL3 6BT

Copyright © St Paul Publications 1984
First published in Great Britain January 1984
Typeset by Academic Typesetting Service, Gerrards Cross
Printed by Billing & Son, Worcester
ISBN 085439 231 9 (paperback)
ISBN 085439 232 7 (hardbound)

St Paul Publications is an activity of the priests and brothers
of the Society of St Paul and of the Daughters of St Paul who
promote the Christian message through the mass media.

Contents

SECTION THREE: THE PILGRIM'S SECRET

SECTION FOUR: THE PILGRIM'S TASKS

To be a pilgrim — John Bunyan

Who would true valour see
Let him come hither;
One here will constant be,
Come wind, come weather;
There's no discouragement
Shall make him once relent
His first avow'd intent
    To be a pilgrim.

About this book

This book has the sub-title 'A Spiritual Notebook'. That best describes its nature. It is the spiritual notebook of a pilgrim. It is concerned with the spiritual life, its principles and practice, and with the Church's doctrine in general as well. This book has been made up mainly from formal speeches, addresses, parish homilies and notes prepared for different occasions, but some parts have been specially written. It does tend to have the limitations of any collection of occasional writings and of the spoken word. The written word, for example, is more polished (or should be) than the writing up of the spoken word. Many of the passages of the book belong to this latter category. And there are repetitions, ideas outlined but not developed, different versions of Scripture used, and doubtless other shortcomings as well. It is not a book meant to be read consecutively from cover to cover. It can be picked up and thought about, in any order and as the individual pleases.

There is another point. As we grow older, we tend, I think, to be helped and inspired by fewer ideas than at an earlier period. Some 'thoughts' have become, over the years, familiar and treasured friends. They have served in the past; they are important now. We go back to them again and again for our own sakes. If we have to speak or write, they will be our subject.

So the pilgrim on his spiritual journey will jot down in his notebook what interests and attracts him most. He has his own way of looking at spirituality. He accepts, of course, all the wise guidance of the masters of the spiritual life, but real assent is probably given only to a part of their teaching, without denying the rest.

There are signposts, too, on the way, put there by the teaching authority of the Church, to prevent our straying from the path that leads to the truth we cannot discover for ourselves. The bishop must take note of these signposts and point them out to the other pilgrims. This book speaks of that teaching as well.

These thoughts are being published as one way of fulfilling the role of a bishop as teacher. It would have been good to have written a book that covered all the important points of the spiritual life and of the Church's doctrine. That has not been possible. This book is incomplete and not too systematic – just the thoughts of one pilgrim to help some of the others.

*   *   *

To be a Pilgrim would never have been published had it not been for the painstaking and devoted work done by Heather Craufurd and Monsignor George Leonard. Father John Crowley played an important part too. And I must not forget the secretaries at Archbishop's House who, amidst other duties, cheerfully coped with this additional burden.

The Pilgrim's Tale

There were many travellers in Judea and Galilee on that first Christmas night, for a census of the people had to be made. Places to lodge were scarce. Some, the poor ones, had no more than a cave or a stable in which to shelter and rest from the fatigue of their long journey. Others were still on the road, they were men in search. Three men, pilgrims these, were in search of a king – one, they said, who would be born at this time and to whom they would be led by a star. Where that star would lead them and what exactly they would find, they were none too certain. They asked questions and sought guidance. The light from the star in the heavens would be their guide, and they sought too that inner light which is what wise men will always seek.

The pilgrim through life's journey needs light for guidance along the road that leads to our true and final home. That pilgrim is you, and that pilgrim is me, often confused and often wounded. Let me tell you about one such pilgrim, neither rich nor poor, not learned yet not foolish, an ordinary person like you and me. He spoke to me about himself and it is he who tells this tale:

"I had been a pilgrim on the journey through life", he told me, "but when I set out on that journey the world seemed young. I did not know how long my journey would be. I did not know the way I should go nor what I should find at the end of the road. My mind was restless with youthful dreams, and my desires strong. I wanted to find peace for my mind, an end to the anguish of the questions I could not answer and yet could not evade. I wished to find the end of all desiring and sought to possess so I would desire no more. I'd heard it said that my mind could not rest until it knew all things and the reason for all things, and I was told of treasures I could possess and my wayward heart would ache no more. They told me the name of these treasures; they called the knowledge of all things and the reasons for them – *truth*, and the object of all my desiring – *goodness*. I could not grasp the meaning of these words 'truth' and 'goodness', strange words which failed to stir me.

"I set out in search, uncertain and confused. What is that truth, I said, which will explain all things to me, what is that goodness which will satisfy now and for-ever? Wise men told me that one was called meaning, the other happiness. I thought further and understood that to know truth and the reason for all things would make me see the meaning of my life and the lives of other people. Then I saw that to search out and to possess good in all its forms gave happiness, and that the best of these was love, and I saw deep within me that I was seeking to love and be loved, and in a manner that was complete and without end. Where would I find, I asked, that most lovable of all persons, the one who would consume my unlimited desire to love? Where would I discover the meaning of all things? As I went on seeking I feared that this happiness, this love and this understanding of the meaning of things, could never be, either here or in another place, now or later on. I thought they were but dreams to soften the nightmare of frustration that robs today of its innocent joys and tomorrow of its bliss. I did not think they could be mine".

My friend went on: "I met others who had set out on the same road. I listened to what they had to say. They told me what they had found out about the meaning of things, about people, about happiness, and they said to me:

'Listen to us. All you can ever know is what you can see around you, what you can touch with your hand and hear with your ears; the rest is nothing but dreams. Do not allow your mind to fret. Do not lose your wits by asking questions that have no answers. There is no real meaning to be understood. Take what you can of the fleeting joys that come your way. Seize them, make them yours, and think no more. Your own experiences are true for you, and these alone. There is nothing else. Stay in the world of unknowing with doubt as your friend'.

"I looked at these travellers and saw them content and at ease. They seemed to have ceased their search. Some had all they needed, fine clothes and a full table. Others had fame, for many knew and esteemed them. Some had power over others. These men, I thought, have found what I was seeking. They do not worry about the meaning of things and persons. Doubt and unknowing have become congenial companions for they no longer ask questions that might disturb, and they are honoured by other travellers and sometimes envied. The good which riches and power gave them, these suffice. What need of more?

"But I saw others on the way. They were neither honoured nor esteemed. They seemed to be sorely wounded. Some were blind, some deaf and could not speak, others lame. They looked, many of them, lean and hungry. The journey was hard for them, or so it seemed, and I wondered what they hoped to find at the end of their journey. They were, I thought, much to be pitied.

"I pondered on all these things, with pity for those who were poor, and some disdain for those who seemed to have found what I half expected I might find at the end of my journey. But I found myself faring no better than the others. I was still in search, sometimes hesitating, walking with doubt, and seizing with relief the fleeting joys as the rich and powerful travellers did. Then my mood would change. The sky would darken and I was like the poor pilgrims, destitute and deprived, though I had a coat upon my back and my step was firm enough, except when it faltered. Within and deep down, I searched and there was nothing, a terrible void. I yearned and did not know for what I yearned. I struggled to understand, yet did not know what it was that I wished to understand. I stood by the wayside and waited, grasping at the present for I feared the future. I still hoped I would find a way that would lead at last to where truth abides and love is real. I hoped and doubted, and the two were one in my divided self. It was dark outside for it was winter, and it was darker still within. The sun had set, and I had neither warmth nor light – no star to guide me on my way".

As my friend, the pilgrim, told his tale, I saw the anguish in his face, for the memory of his journey through life, when the sun did not shine, haunted him still in the telling of it. But now, as I gazed, his expression slowly changed as grief yielded to peace. He took up his story again:

"It was then, in the shadow and darkness of winter, I saw in silhouette against the sky, the form of another pilgrim. He did not follow our road as the other pilgrims did. He came the other way, but he seemed to come from the land of dawn to which we, the wounded ones, were going. I wondered even if he might now bring news of another land, the one to which we were making our way. I did not know. I saw from time to time that he would stop before a pilgrim who was lame; he would speak and the cripple stood and then walked with a new strength, a fresh vigour in his limbs. He would touch the eyes of a blind pilgrim who, like the cripple, now walked on, his darkness turned to light. He would hold out his hand to a deaf pilgrim who could then hear and set out again on his journey singing, when before he had been silent.

"The Stranger looked upon the rich traveller, and I could see that the Stranger was sad, for he saw that the rich man had so much and yet so little. The Stranger would gaze in wonder at those with power, for it seemed they did not know what they could do, what they could command. Yet I saw that he looked at them, the rich and the powerful, with the same pity, the same love, as he looked upon the poor and the destitute. They seemed, all of them, like sheep with no shepherd to guide and help them along the way.

"I felt drawn to this mysterious Stranger, this pilgrim so like, and yet so unlike us. His face was kindly and welcoming, his eyes clear and fine; they seemed to see further and deeper into the secret recesses of the minds of those with whom he spoke. But I saw something else in those eyes. It seemed they had looked upon something so great that it could not be described, or at least not well. I thought too that he must have looked upon some great beauty, for in his eyes were admiration and awe, the kind of wonder that children know when their gaze has looked on some new and wondrous thing. There was something more. He was, I thought, a man without desire, as if he possessed all, although from what I saw he seemed to have so little. Here was a man, I thought, a complete man, whole and wholesome.

"I came to him, for his very presence drew me to his side. I felt suddenly so very small, a strange fear gripped me. I wanted to run away and leave him. I feared to lose my freedom, for I did not know what he might ask of me. I preferred to loiter along the pilgrim way with that odd mixture of hope that I would reach home at the end of my journey, and fear that I might not. But I did not wish to be led. I would walk alone, my own strength would be enough. I did not wish to yield to this love which I knew was forcing me to give myself to him.

"He spoke first and asked me where I was going, and what did I want. 'I'm not sure', I replied. But when I paused to think, I realised that I wished to know the meaning of all things, and that happiness which is so complete and which has no end. *Then* I shall rest and shall have discovered myself.

'Why then', he answered, 'you must come and follow me. I shall show you the way that will take you to that city for which you are destined. There you will discover the meaning of all things. You will know truth. You will have happiness which is complete and without end. You will know love. You will be loved by One who, of all lovers, is the most loving. You will be united with the One who, above all others, is the most lovable. That is ecstasy, the endless now of unending bliss. You will have reached the end of your pilgrim journey. You will have discovered yourself, for you are made to know truth and to love'.

As the Stranger spoke, I warmed to him and to what he had to say. He did not speak as others do. He spoke of things he had seen and as I listened to his words my desire to listen further and to remain by his side grew stronger. I said to him: 'Let us remain here in this spot, let us make this our dwelling'. But it could not be. He would, he said, give me some taste of future joys, but the fulness of them could not yet be mine. I must keep walking ever onwards through that pilgrimage which is life. Joys and sorrows would continue to compete for the mastery of my heart, light and darkness wrestling in my mind.

"We spoke on. I said: 'He who is above all the most lovable, he who will explain all things and who is in some manner the explanation of all that is, is not this what they call God?' The Stranger smiled, a smile that spoke approval and delight. Encouraged now, I spoke on. 'If there is a God, then He would be my Father too, and Father of all who journey on through life'. The Stranger answered:

> 'Why are you so fearful that there might be a God, and one who has concern for you and wishes you well? What is it that you want? Would you prefer a world in which the lives of the pilgrims have no true meaning? Where happiness is fleeting and often defeated by pain and sorrow?
>
> Would you not wish rather that the meaning of things and the purpose of them is in part now hidden from you, but shall in the end become clear? The choice is between the Mystery and the Absurd'.

'If I choose the Mystery', I said, 'am I not moving into a world of dreams, of illusions, escaping from what is real?'

> 'No, it is not so. To embrace the Mystery is to discover the real. It is to walk towards the light, to glimpse the morning star, to catch sight from time to time of what is truly real'.

'Speak more', I said, 'about that light'. The Stranger said:

> 'It is no more than a flicker of light through the cloud of unknowing; a fitful ray of light that is a messenger from the sun that is hidden from your gaze. You see the light but not the sun. When you glimpse the light and set yourself to look more closely, then you will begin to see some sense in the darkness that surrounds you. Your eyes will begin to pick out the shape of things. You will begin to see in things and persons around you the presence of the One who gives them meaning and purpose, and that it is He who is the explanation of them all. Now perhaps you begin to realise, the One of whom I speak is my Father. We call Him God, for so He is'.

I was puzzled, perhaps even shocked, for these were strange words, ideas beyond my understanding. 'Show me the Father', I said, 'that is all I ask'. The Stranger measured his every word:

> 'Whoever has seen me, has seen the Father. You must believe that I am in the Father, and the Father is in me'.

Then like a flash of lightning I understood. I saw with new eyes and clearly that this was indeed the Son of the Father whom they call God.

"The Stranger was a stranger no more, for when friendship grows, the sense of distance goes; faith and trust take the place of doubt and hesitation. Now, in that lightning flash, I could see the way that would lead to all truth and all love, and would lead to Him who simply is, and from whom I and all the other pilgrims came, and to whom we are destined to return and in whom was to be found the purpose of every human life. And I knew something else, and with great certainty and peace, that His Son would walk with us, or rather we with him, for the rest of time. He would not only show us the manner of our going, but was himself the way, for he had truth from which he spoke, and life which he could share. He had come along our pilgrim way to find us and give us guidance, to restore our sight, to cure our deafness, and give vigour to our crippled limbs. Now we could match his pace; following him, and with peace in our hearts, pick our way through the dangers and turmoils which would be ours in this restless world through which we must travel. I understood now; God himself had become a pilgrim in His Son Jesus Christ.

"So there is meaning in our journey. We in search of God, and God in search of us. God, in Jesus Christ, spoke indeed of things I could not see or touch, and with words which dispelled the darkness of my mind and brought warmth to the coldness of my heart. I saw clearly that the Stranger who had become my friend was himself God who had become man. The Son of God had become the Son of man. My mind could hardly receive the truth, so great and so wondrous was it. In his presence I was overcome. I knelt and could but say: 'Depart from me for I am a sinful man'. What once did seem absurd to me now dawned upon my mind as real and true. I knew, but my senses had not told me. Other voices spoke, and they were speaking and commanding in ways that were strange and unknown. It was the voice of him who knows and loves, and came in search of us. It was a light that pierced the darkness of my mind and gave me strength to see.

"He took my hand and raised me up. He looked at me and I knew that he wanted me to follow him. I said: 'Yes, Lord, where you will and as you will, lead me on and let it be in darkness if that is your wish. Enough for me to know that it is you who will be my guide'. I knew forgiveness at that moment and felt a new vigour within me. I felt strong and knew that I could follow him and for every moment of time. I would still search, but knew now what it was I was seeking – life without end and love beyond my dreams. In him I would find these things".

My friend now left me and I walked home alone. As I went I saw at the side of the road a group of plaster figures; a man and a woman, some shepherd boys and three wise men, and in a manger a baby wrapped in swaddling clothes. I glanced at the hedge in which the crib was set and looked up at the church which towered high above it. I walked towards it, entered and remained, silent and alone, to refresh myself before once again taking to the road. I prayed and it came to me that the Stranger about whom my friend had spoken was that small child wrapped in swaddling clothes. I said: "Glory to God in the highest, peace to men of good will". I marvelled at what my friend had said and pondered long upon it. I too, like my friend, had encountered the Stranger and believed.

['The Pilgrim's Tale' was originally broadcast by the Cardinal on BBC Radio. It is reproduced here by their kind permission.]

The way of the Pilgrim

Life is a pilgrimage. We are on the march, and sooner or later we shall reach our destination. That destination we call heaven. There we shall see God as He is, and that experience will be the cause of a happiness which will be complete and have no end. We are made for that.

While on the road we cannot help wondering about God. What is He like? What does He want for us? What does He expect of us? And sometimes we ask whether He exists at all. So many of our fellow pilgrims have decided that there is no God; others just go through life doubting or not knowing. But the important questions still require answers. What happens after death? Nothing? Has life no meaning? Are we only part of an absurd situation devoid of sense and purpose?

If only we could see God, life would be very different; our uncertainties would go and we should take each step in life, clear about the direction and firm in our tread. There would be no faltering, no confusion. But it is not like that. Furthermore, apart from our inability to see God with our eyes or hear His voice with our ears, there is, in addition, the problem that, as pilgrims, we are weak and wounded. We do not function as we should.

There are times when we seem to respond to what we know is expected of us. There are other times when we falter badly. We get tied up with all kinds of things that distract us from thinking about the end of the journey, or delay us on the way, indeed entice us to go in the wrong direction altogether. We are sinners, always in danger of going wrong.

Moreover, there is a great deal of pain and suffering. That can slow the pace. Many simply cannot cope and some, indeed, suffer so much that they cannot believe that there is someone who loves them and wants them to reach the destination, where all things will be well. When we have acknowledged the existence of that 'Someone' and learned that He has intervened in our affairs, we should begin to respond. We want to find out more about Him, try to be in touch with Him, and then discover that we should obey Him and serve Him. We have come to recognise that in God are to be found the ultimate meaning and purpose of all things, and especially of ourselves. This response is what we call 'the spiritual life'.

If we do not have a spiritual life, then our living is impoverished. Important questions remain unanswered; life itself will appear to be pointless, and we have no future to which to look forward. But we are made "to know God, to love Him and serve Him in this world, and to be happy with Him for ever in the next". This is the point of the pilgrimage.

* * *

Knowing God

If only we could see God - that wish, deep in the hearts of countless men and women down the ages, inspired the prayer of a notable Old Testament pilgrim. Moses prayed: "Show me your glory, I beg you" (Exod 33,18). But he was told: "You cannot see My face, for man cannot see Me and live". "You must stand on the rock", Moses was told, "and when My glory passes by, I will put you in a cleft of the rock and shield you with My hand while I pass by. Then I shall take My hand away and you shall see the back of Me; but My face is not to be seen" (ibid. v. 22–23).

We cannot see God, but we can catch glimpses of His 'glory'. What is that 'glory'?, the Shekinah to which reference is made so often in the Bible?

"The glory (of God) reflects abundance of good and truth, the power that acts in nature and history. The whole earth is full of His glory. It does not mean that the glory fills the earth in the way in which ether fills space or water fills the ocean. It means that the whole earth is full of His presence . . . the whole earth is full of His glory. The outwardness of the world communicates something of the indwelling greatness of God. . .".

(*God in Search of Man* by Abraham Joshua Heschel, 1955, pp. 82, 83. Farrar Strauss & Co., New York)

It is, then, through persons and things that we can glimpse something of His 'glory'. This, after all, is the teaching of St Paul: "From the foundations of the world men have caught sight of His invisible nature, His eternal power and His divineness, as they are known through His creatures" (Rom 1,20). The goodness, truth and beauty, which we know and love in persons and things, speak to us of these attributes or qualities as they are in God. And power in all its forms tells of the One from whom all power comes and upon whom it depends here and now for its effects.

Goodness, truth, beauty and power in the created universe are different manifestations of the glory of God, the Creator. He shows His power in many different ways, in the forces of nature, in the strength and skill of humans, in machines of every kind. He reveals His goodness and beauty in all that is lovely and desirable. His mind is explored as we go in pursuit of truth. C.S. Lewis explained it thus: "I was learning the far more secret doctrine that pleasures are shafts of the glory as it strikes our sensibility. As it impinges on our wills or understanding, we give it different names – goodness or truth or the like. But its flash upon our senses and mood is pleasure. But aren't there bad, unlawful pleasures? Certainly there are. But in calling them 'bad pleasures' I take it we are using a kind of shorthand. We mean, 'pleasures snatched by unlawful act'. It is the stealing of the apple that is bad, not the sweetness. The sweetness is still a beam from the glory. That does not palliate the stealing. It makes it worse. There is sacrilege in the theft. We have abused a holy thing" (C.S. Lewis: Letters to Malcolm, p. 117). It is good to realise that God is present everywhere. In Him we live and move and have our being. His presence is manifested to us through His creation, and in our reflection and enjoyment of it we are in touch with Him. It is good to realise too that, at any moment, we may just rest in the thought of God's presence here and now. God speaks through His creation, but He speaks too through stillness and silence. And if we cannot find that silence because of the noise which surrounds us, we must look for it inside ourselves. In that silence He may invite us to pursue further our search for Him.

We do not see Him as He is. Crouched in the cleft of a rock we catch glimpses of His presence, when something of His glory is manifested to us in His creation. But for us to know Him more intimately, He must speak and tell us about Himself. In Old Testament times the people of God, His chosen people, meditated on Him and on His intervention in their affairs. All this is recorded, and is done so for our benefit. God uses these records and meditations as a way of speaking to us, they are God's Word. But if "in former days, God spoke to our fathers in many ways and by many means, through the prophets", wrote the author of the letter to the Hebrews, "now at last in these times He has spoken to us with a Son to speak for Him; a Son who is the radiance of his Father's splendour and the full expression of his being" (Heb 1,1-3).

The Word has become flesh and dwelt amongst us. It is now no longer just a question of listening to the Word of God as contained in the Old Testament writings; a person has come among us, and that person is God made man. Hence the importance of that passage in St John's gospel which records a conversation between Our Lord and the apostle Philip. Jesus had said: "If you had learned to recognise me, you would have learned to recognise my Father too. From now onwards you are to recognise Him; you have seen Him"; Philip did not understand, so he said: "Lord, let us see the Father, and then we shall be satisfied". The Lord then said, and very solemnly: "Have I been with you all this time, Philip, and you still do not know me? To have seen me is to have seen the Father, so how can you say 'Let us see the Father'? Do you not believe that I am in the Father, and the Father is in me?" (Jn 14,6–10).

We can know something of the divine by looking at creation; we can learn about God from the Old Testament writings. But our knowledge and understanding derived from these sources is limited. Our capacity to understand is itself small. Neither our ideas nor our images are in any way adequate to express the truth about God. I once read an author who wrote about our idea or picture of God being constructed "out of the fragments of our experiences". He called it a "crude, childish representation at the best". I am not certain that I would wish to go as far as that. In any case in the person of Jesus Christ, true God and true man, we have translated for us into human terms facts about God which otherwise we could not know. God has had pity on our limitations. He has spoken to us through His Son, the image of the invisible God, the "true likeness of the God we cannot see" (Col 1,15). Attitudes and actions of Jesus Christ described in the Gospels reveal to us in a unique and wonderful manner the secrets of God's own life. We can see, for instance, what people, weak and wounded, mean to God. The compassion and mercy shown by Our Lord are the revelation of God's love for us, His mercy and His compassion. Every word of Jesus Christ comes to us with the authority of God Himself.

The lovely and encouraging things about God revealed to us in and by Our Lord are not the whole of the revelation. There are stern lessons too, and warnings. We must see the whole, not just the parts that please.

Moses had prayed: "Show me your glory, I beg you". How he would have loved to have read St John when he wrote: "And the Word was made flesh, he lived among us; and we saw His glory, the glory that is His as the

only Son of the Father, full of grace and truth" (Jn
1,14). Indeed, goodness, beauty, truth and power have
become incarnated. Through Him who is the way, the
truth and the life, we derive the inspiration and the
strength to keep going on our pilgrim way.

*   *   *

Loving God

We have been told that we must love God. "Thou shalt
love the Lord thy God with thy whole heart and with
thy whole soul and with thy whole mind. This is the
greatest and first commandment. And the second is
like to this: Thou shalt love thy neighbour as thyself"
(Mt 22,37-39). The spiritual lives of too many people
are based on fear. Now I would not wish to minimise
the importance of a wholesome filial fear of God.
Fear of hell is, on occasions, no bad motive for avoiding sin. Furthermore, our task is to be pleasing to
God and this means that we must keep the commandments, and do what He expects of us. Morality is
important, and not only as an end in itself. It should be
the test of our intent to love God and serve Him. We
should be fearful lest in breaking His law we displease
Him. There can be no serious spiritual life which ignores
obedience to God. That is evident.

   It would, however, be an impoverished spiritual life
which was not based on trying to love God. After all,
that is the first commandment. Fear is an exhausting
emotion. Love must cast out fear, eventually. But I
believe that it takes most of us quite a long time to
learn about the love of God. It dawns slowly.

   Many of us feel quite uneasy because we have to
admit that we do not love God, or certainly not in any

manner that is familiar to us. It is helpful to remember
that wanting to love God may well be as far as we can
go: "Yes, I would like to love God, but . . .". That is
already to have gone a long way. In human relationships
it is often after we have discovered another person's
love or regard for us, that we then begin to warm to
that person. This is most certainly true in our relationship with God, and we have St John's authority for it
(1 Jn 4,10). So, when we discover from our reading,
praying or experience of life, that God loves us, then we
shall be affected. We begin to want to love Him in
return. A pilgrimage into the mystery of the love which
He is has begun.

We have to understand that 'loving' is essentially a
divine experience. The prototype of all loving is the way
God loves. When humans love they are, as it were,
copying God or, more accurately, are doing 'something'
which is characteristic of God. That is why our experiences of love can tell us something about God's love for
us. It may be the realisation of a parent's love, or friendship, or falling in love. These enable us to explore more
deeply the meaning of St John's words: "God is love"
(1 Jn 4,16). Our experiences of loving are no more than
a hint of the way love is in God. Whatever we find best
in love is in Him. Love belongs to God. We hold it in
trust, His gift to us.

We have to hang on to the fact of God's love for us.
That demands courage and tenacity. There is so much in
the world that seems to contradict the whole idea of a
loving God; there is enough in our own lives to make us
doubt it. No one has ever given a totally satisfactory
explanation of why there is evil, and so suffering, in life,
at least not to my way of thinking. But there are truths
which point us in the right direction. They will indicate
where a solution is to be found. First, we are sinners. We
are free. We have to be free in order to be able to love
truly. We misuse that freedom, individually and collec-
tively, so there is tragedy, suffering and death. Secondly,
there is the fact that God became man, accepted the
human condition (except for sin) and gave it a new

significance and value. We shall return often to this theme in the notes that follow. Thirdly, we have to hang on all the time to the fact that God loves us, and this in every crisis and however much events and facts appear to contradict the truth. We must trust God. It is very easy to trust when the evidence for doing so is obvious; it is quite different when it is not. God asks us, sometimes often, to go on with the pilgrimage through life in the dark, but always trusting. Trust is a proof of love.

This theme, God's love for us, and ours for Him, will occur often in this book. And this should not be surprising, for we are made to love God. That is what we are for. Learning how to do it is an essential part of the spiritual life. Indeed we might say that it is the point of the whole exercise.

*   *   *

Serving God

We are to serve God. How we do this will depend on each one's personal vocation. God calls us to serve Him in different ways. One factor is common to all of us. Everything human, except sin, has a new significance since God became man. Jesus Christ lived the ordinary life of a carpenter of his day in Nazareth, and by doing so he has made holy all ordinary things and activities. When you work, for example, the Father is reminded of the fact that His divine Son once worked too; when you sit around chatting to friends, the Father remembers that His Son did the same. This may sound just a bit naive on a first reading, but think about it. It is an idea rich in consequences, for it means that whatever we do (except, always, what is sinful) looks different to the Father than it does to us. You have that floor to sweep. Nothing very dramatic in that. God sees more than the sweeping. He sees it as a service of Him, and this because His Son did that kind of thing for thirty years of his life. Almost nothing has been recorded of those years lived by Our Lord in the family at Nazareth. As news value they are of no consequence, but where it truly matters those years are precious indeed. And so it is for all of you. Your daily work is your daily service of God. To make that service a loving one adds to it, both in giving honour to God and in the joy you will experience.

The more we get to know God, and the greater our understanding of His love for us becomes, the more easily does our service through ordinary tasks become deeply satisfying. It will not stop work from being burdensome, boring and frustrating at times. The satisfaction comes from it being a loving service of God; in itself the task to be done may be unspeakably dull. Much of our work is.

When we think of our lives in terms of service of God, we cannot, must not, neglect the second commandment. We have to love our neighbour as ourselves. It is important to be clear about our responsibilities and duties in respect of other people. Our spiritual lives are not ways of being comfortable, of finding peace and joy for ourselves only. Our striving for union with God is a personal and private matter no doubt. But the Gospel command to love other people is very clear. And this does not mean just having a vague sense of goodwill towards people. It involves not only wishing good things for other people, but helping them to obtain them. It will involve action. Would you leave a man to die starving in the street outside your home, while you remain within reading the Bible and praying? That contrast is perhaps expressed too brutally, but it makes a telling point; the first and second commandments are not easily separated. St John puts it clearly enough: "Let us therefore love God, because God first hath loved us. If any man say 'I love God', and hateth his brother whom he seeth, how can he love God whom he seeth not? And this commandment we have from God, that he who loveth God love also his brother" (1 Jn 4,19–21).

Obeying the command to love our neighbour is, like the command to love God, an instruction on how to function properly as a human being. Hating other people, hurting them, neglecting their needs – that is inhuman behaviour. We are less than human when we treat others in an inhuman manner. St Matthew records how Our Lord spoke about the day of judgment when the criterion to qualify for the kingdom of God was our treatment of the hungry, the thirsty, the naked, the prisoner, the stranger (Mt 25,31–46). And the important point was made, namely to feed the hungry or to give drink to the thirsty, is to do it to Christ himself. We shall not in this life ever understand the full significance of that. But it does indicate the unity that exists between all humans in Christ. In each of us the Father sees reflected the face of His Son; so we too should see Christ in each other.

There are men and women all over the world who have dedicated their lives to obeying the teaching given in that twenty-fifth chapter of St Matthew. They are truly living the Gospel. There are many, too, who do not know the Gospel and yet devote themselves to serving the poor in their needs. Our Lord has a word for them. "When was it that we saw thee sick or in prison and came to thee?", they asked. "Believe me, when you did it to one of these my least brethren, you did it unto me" (Mt 25,39–40). They have served Christ in their neighbour although, without the eyes of faith, they had not seen his presence in them.

The neighbours that I am required to love are, of course, my family, those who live in my area, those I meet at work. But is that all? A keen sense of the bond which our common humanity creates is part of that second commandment, and so, therefore, the interests and fate of all peoples in some manner are my concern. What have I in mind? I think first of much poverty in the world, and the fate of all those persons who are dying of hunger this very day, and especially of the children. I have in mind those innumerable wars of this century, and not least of the present decade, with the

suffering that they bring. I recall all those people who
suffer violence at the hands of others, those who have
sacrificed their freedom for the sake of conscience, those
whose dignity as human beings has been brutally as-
saulted. I reflect too on the madness which has led us to
invent nuclear bombs and to threaten to use them.
Could human folly go further than this? Would not the
dropping of such a bomb, however justified it might
seem, be the ultimate in wickedness?

In our age, so sophisticated and so talented, we have
not as yet tamed the barbarian in us. We can be crude
and cruel. We are too little surprised at the enormity
and sinfulness of man's cruelty to man. We have become
hardened to it. Repression, torture, denial of human
rights are part of modern life. We are neither wiser nor
better than our forefathers. If the christian philosophy
of life based on respect and love for God and for our
neighbours had been embraced and practised throughout
the world, then the terrible crimes of our age could
never have been perpetrated. The command of the
Lord, then, "to repent and believe the Gospel" speaks in
our day with perhaps an even greater insistence than it
did in the time of Our Lord. If the Gospel be the truth
about God and how we should relate to Him (which
indeed it is), we should listen to what He has to say. If
there be sin in the world (and there is) then we need to
repent.

Now this repentance has two parts: our expression of
sorrow for sins committed, and a change of heart away
from sin to God. It is to that change of heart that we are
constantly being called. A change of heart can be sudden
and traumatic, as was the case with St Paul, or more
usually it is a life-long process. It involves a decision to
change, a struggle to live in accordance with that decision, much failure and a constant willingness to start all
over again. Our part is to try; success is a gift from God.
It is the will to go on trying – itself His gift – which
matters most, for that continuous effort is proof of our
love, or rather of our wanting to love.

We shall never overcome the tendency to sin within

us. There will always be a struggle. Fear of the consequences of grave sin is an admirable motive for avoiding
sin, as I have already said. But we need higher and better
motives: to be inspired by a vision of what is in store for
us after life, and which can be experienced in some
measure here and now. That is why a life spent in trying
to love God and our neighbour will be a happy life, and
happy in proportion as we become more selfless. The
wounded and the weak among us limp along, but deep
down we can be at peace for we know that His love for
us is stronger than our neglect of Him. If we walk
away from Him deliberately we condemn ourselves to
ultimate misery and isolation.

On the way to God

A Pilgrim's thoughts

There are certain words which I find to be very expressive
of the way that I think about life. Pilgrim is one such,
searching or seeking is another.

I think of myself as a pilgrim through life. I came
from nothing, I shall be here some sixty, seventy or
possibly more years, and then I shall no longer be here.
My stay here has a clear beginning and a definite end. It
seems clear, and it becomes increasingly clearer, that I
do not belong to this world, well, at least, not perma-
nently. What I am and do when I am here is important,
no doubt, but I do not remain. I move on; I am a
pilgrim. Well, am I? Suppose that there is nothing at
the end of life, only total extinction. Can I be said to be
a pilgrim? Pilgrims are on their way to some place; there
is a destination. I would find it very hard to accept that
after life on this earth there is no more 'me', and nothing for me; no more 'you', and nothing for you. It
would not make sense of life, and no sense of death.

And what about all the hopes and expectations that
I have about life? Is there to be no future realisation of
them? What about all the people, in fact the vast majority
of mankind, for whom life is excessively difficult for
lack of health, lack of food, lack of freedom? Is it all
that life has to offer? No, everything that is in me cries
out for the need to reach a destination where there will
be no more tears or pain, and where all my deepest
aspirations and desires will be finally and completely
satisfied. The thought of arriving at the place where all
these things will be, and the thought of Someone who
will put it all right, that can keep me going. Every

pilgrim cheerfully puts up with the journey when the going is rough, precisely because there is something to look forward to at the end of it. I shall have found what I have been searching for.

There is that word 'searching'. It is very much a monk's word and recalls that the raison d'être of every monastic vocation is 'to seek God', as the Rule of St Benedict says. I am in search. I am trying to understand the ultimate purpose of my life, the meaning of it, and the meaning of everything and everybody else. I want to know why I am here and what I am for. It would be hard to establish answers to these questions by a survey of public opinion. We are, as a society, confused, distracted, uninterested, in fact lost. But the idea of searching can be stood on its head. It helps if we switch from the notion of our searching for God and instead think about God coming to find us, for after all that is the way it is. It is we who are lost. It is God who is looking for us. He wants us in a warm and intimate way, even when we feel that we do not need Him.

A pilgrim wanders through life, often limping, sometimes bewildered, at times quite lost; and the pilgrim is searching, often quite unconsciously, for something or someone to make sense of life, and certainly to make sense of death. He or she may discover that God has spoken in many ways but most emphatically through a Son, whom to see is to have seen the Father Himself. I need to dwell on certain experiences which can lead me to catch just a glimpse of God (in a manner of speaking). These experiences are foretastes of something that will be mine one day, hints of realities that cannot be known through my senses but are nonetheless true.

I argue first from beauty. If I see something truly beautiful or hear something very beautiful, my mind is raised up and my heart may be warmed. I want to hang on to that moment, savour it, keep it and make it mine. At times I shall want to cry out in admiration and delight, by clapping or by cheering or perhaps in song. Then the moment passes and I mourn the impermanence of the experience. I await another. I reflect: if only I could see or hear something which is even more beautiful, that would be a further joy; and what an experience it would be if I could know that which among the most beautiful things was the most beautiful of them all. That would be the highest of all the experiences of joy, and total fulfilment. The most beautiful of all things I call God. At this point I should attempt a learned explanation as to why I believe that this most beautiful of all things, or persons, in fact truly exists. I am not too certain that I can; it has as much to do with instinct as with reason.

I argue secondly from the experience of loving. When I speak of love I mean something very noble, very deep, and very pure. When I love someone, and love that person very much, then I want to hang on to that. I do not want to lose my loving or my beloved. I want it to go on forever and to give me a happiness which is total and which shall have no end. But it never works out that way. It passes, and I then realise that the greatest experience of loving will not be now in this life, but later on. Meanwhile, I go on looking and longing for that which is the most lovable of all. I call that which is the most lovable, God.

So here I am, a pilgrim through life, restless indeed, looking, searching all the time for that which will make me truly and fully myself. That is natural, and I discover that it is only when I can delight in that which is most beautiful, in that which is the fullness of goodness, and only when I am united to that which is most lovable that I am truly myself and so truly human.

I am made to sing out with joy at that which is most beautiful and to love that which is most lovable. I am made for God, whom to see is to contemplate the most beautiful of all; whom to love is to love the most lovable. Yes, I am made for God, and I am foolish indeed if I do not understand that. It is my duty, and should with practice and perseverance become my joy, to praise Him and serve Him.

The way is often rough for a pilgrim and hard going,

but pilgrims must keep going resolutely and courageously. They are lost if they stop looking for the right
way to reach their destination. But there is one who is
on the look-out to guide us: it is the Son of God who is
the way, the truth and the life.

*   *   *   *   *

As we climb the mountain

There is a very lovely story in the Book of Kings. It
concerns the prophet Elijah. It is not, as far as I know,
a very well known story. That is a pity.

Things were going badly for Elijah. His life was
threatened. He was afraid. He was on the run from his
pursuers. He grew weary, not just physically weary, but
he was weighed down by the burden of life. He stretched
himself out under a juniper tree. "Lord, I have had
enough", he said, "take my life, I am no better than my
ancestors". Then he went off to sleep. As he slept an
angel touched him and told him to get up and eat the
food that was there for him, a scone baked on hot
stones and a jar of water. Elijah went back to sleep, but
eventually got up and ate and drank, and strengthened
by that food walked forty days and nights until he
reached Horeb, the mountain of God. It was there on
the mountain that he experienced the presence of God.

There came a mighty wind so strong that it tore
the mountain and shattered the rocks, but God was not
in the wind. After the wind there came an earthquake
and after the earthquake there was fire, but God was
not in the fire. After the fire there came the sound of a
gentle breeze. On this occasion God's presence was
made known to Elijah by the gentle breeze; he knew
that God was there and spoke to Him of what lay

deepest in his heart, and he affirmed his determination to give glory to God and serve Him.

Sometimes, in the life of a person, God enters in a dramatic way, unsuspected, unannounced, suddenly, like a storm breaking in after a period of calm. Or He comes like a great wind that uproots trees, lashes the sea and buffets the ships that are on it. It happened like that to St Paul on his way to Damascus. But more often, indeed most often, God's coming is gentler and, maybe, less obvious, like an evening breeze at the end of a sultry day.

As with individuals, so it is with the Church. Great events can shake the Church and much may seem to be destructive; old practices uprooted like worn out trees; the barque of Peter buffeted by the winds of change. A great Council is like that. But in the normal life of the Church it is otherwise. The Spirit moves more gently: like a breeze, not a wind; a soft light, not a glare. It was of course different for the Apostles when the Holy Spirit came down on them. A great wind blew, and tongues of fire, and the effects on them were as dramatic and dazzling as this latest manifestation of God's presence, the descent of the Holy Spirit. They were changed instantly. Transformed from men of little courage and little hope they became fearless and confident. It is not so, normally, for us; rather will it be the gentle breeze, the glow of light, warmth from embers.

From time to time we feel like the prophet Elijah. "Lord, I have had enough, take my life, I am no better than my ancestors". The temptation is to lie down and sleep, protected by that sleep from getting too involved in the life of the Church, or so downcast and over-burdened by the difficulties of life that I can go no further. There is always a messenger from God, an angel to nudge us: "Eat and drink. Receive the Body and Blood of Christ in the Eucharist, for there you will find the food which will help you to walk forty days and nights, and more, to the mountain of God". The day's ration for the day's march on our pilgrim way.

But as we climb to the top of the mountain to the

full vision of God, we should pause from time to time and stop and feel the gentle breeze which is the Spirit of God, the Holy Spirit. God in the Holy Spirit is with us, given to us at Baptism and Confirmation in a special manner.

We need to stop, listen and look. That listening and that looking are prayer.

*   *   *   *   *

Two persons

We are all, in a sense, two persons. This is, of course, in a manner of speaking only. There is the outer person, the one the rest of us pass in the corridor, meet casually, see at work or play. Then there is the inner person, the deep self, the real person, the one that is less easy to know. Acquaintances may make guesses and be more or less right. Friends and relations will know us a little better; some, maybe, very well. But, in fact, only we can know that inner person, the deep self, even if we do not always understand ourselves fully.

We may be frightened to look too closely at that person, for we should be seeing the dark side, the low points, the insecurity, the lack of confidence, disappointments, sadnesses of all kinds, the inner wounds. It is the area where pain is. Then there is the bright side, the high points, the lofty aspirations to be and to achieve, the sensitivity to what is best, to what is most beautiful and most noble, the response to the goodness and lovableness of other people. This is the paradise where we are at peace and happy.

Yet we experience a conflict between the bright and the dark, between the best that we want, and what we know to be less good. How do we resolve it? We look beyond and above ourselves to find that which will totally satisfy, and which we sense will give us dignity and nobility. It is reaching out beyond the confines and restrictions of ordinary human experience.

Such an outreaching has inspired what is best in art and literature. But the artist cannot always express fully what lies deepest, nor can he ever create that perfect expression of beauty which is more beautiful than the beauty he perceives, or more beautiful than his creation can make it. The experience of the artist is to some degree the experience of each one of us. It is deep in all of us if we look closely. It is the need to admire, to gaze in wonder, to be drawn to that which is greater and nobler than ourselves. It is, to put it in other terms, the need to worship and adore.

Fine thoughts about reaching out to Him who is best and most beautiful often ring hollow in our ears. It is because there is the other side, the pain that I know or have known, or the wrong that I do or think, against the honest judgment of my better self. That is another world and I flounder in it, unable to escape.

Every experience of weakness, the consciousness of inner wounds, the adverse judgment of conscience, what are these but the proof that I am not what I should be? They show that I am in need of being healed, of being helped. I am not self-sufficient. To put it in other terms, I need to be saved.

At the very heart of religion there are these two needs, the need to worship and the need to be saved. God became man to enable us to worship the Father in spirit and in truth; He became man to heal our wounds. The Christian discovers, moreover, that God is love, as St John said. It is the lover's role to help and to heal and to get the beloved to respond. It is also the experience of the Christian to discover that the Lord's command to "love the Lord thy God with thy whole heart, thy whole soul and thy whole mind" is not only the law of the New Testament from Our Lord himself, but the law of man's nature. The second commandment follows from the first and it is to love our neighbour as ourselves. That too is the law of God. It is the basis for human living.

When I realise that what is best and most beautiful loves me more profoundly, more intensely than any human being possibly could, then I am consoled and inspired. That is a call to stretch out beyond myself to Him who is greater than I. The knowledge of that love will lead me to gaze in wonder and admiration at His goodness and beauty. It will also bring me peace and happiness. Furthermore, the wounds of the inner person will be healed and the conflict resolved.

Seeking a direction

Groping for the light

We need in our day, in spite of all the knowledge which the world can give us, in spite of all the marvellous advances in our society, to recapture a sense of wonder as we probe the mysteries of God and of His love for us. But we shall never be able to discover any of the secrets about God unless we are humble and small.

The mysteries, which we have been given to reflect upon and make part of our lives, are so much greater, so much beyond our capacity to understand. We are so very small; we are at the foothills in our understanding of God and His world. But it is good that we should be at the foothills; that keeps us humble. Eventually we shall get to the top of the mountain. We shall then see the full vision.

* * *

There is something deep in each one of us which drives us on to search. What it is that we seek we do not always know. It is in part to understand, to know the reason for this pain, that hurt, the loss of one we love, the sickness which we witness, the loneliness which gnaws at the heart, the loss of hope, the despair of doubt. It is fear of the dark.

But there is another part, another urge, one which seeks and craves, craves that all manner of things should be well. It is the search for joy, for peace of mind, for happiness of heart. It is the love of light.

The fear of the dark, the longing for light – foe and

friend of every man – this is the common human experience. The coming of dawn, the rising of the sun, the
passing away of night, precious moments celebrated in
song and poem.

*   *   *

We are apt to fall into the trap of thinking that we are
self-sufficient, that we do not need God, that God is a
concept that belongs to a more primitive people. Yet are
we in our day wiser than our ancestors? We know more,
can achieve more, but are we better at understanding
the true meaning and purpose of every human life? Do
we live more in harmony and peace than by-gone ages?
   The answers to these questions are clear enough.
Maybe if we have come to think of a world without God
as sensible and self-evident, then perhaps we are being as
naive about religion as our forefathers were about the
working of the universe, about science. Every age needs
to be humble about what it does not know, or has
forgotten.

*   *   *

There is a need today, in every profession and in every
walk of life, to rediscover a sense of purpose. I speak of
an ultimate purpose that makes sense, that is one which
corresponds to man's deepest aspirations and needs, or
rather fulfils them. Individuals cannot just muddle
through life without knowing why; nor can a society
survive in peace and serenity unless there is a shared
vision of what man is and what he is for.
   That must include surely a recognition of the need
in each individual of the 'spiritual', of the 'divine';
it includes a respect for life, a striving to ensure that the
dignity of every human be defended and promoted,
and the proper use of our material resources. It means,

in short, having a vision of human existence which we know to be true and which we can all share.

* * * * *

Hunger for God

I have been thinking about the hunger for the things of God. In our public life we move further and further away from God and the things of God, and yet in the hearts of men and women I believe that the yearning for God is becoming more and more intense.

When the first Apostles went out into the streets of Jerusalem at the first Pentecost, they had nothing material to give to the poor and needy. What they had to give was quite different. "Silver and gold I have none", said St Peter, "but what I have I give you; in the name of Jesus of Nazareth, walk". The crippled man, his handicap cured, went leaping into the Temple in order to praise God.

The towns and cities of our land are full of people who do not need our silver and gold, but desperately need to hear the good news of the Gospel. They are lame and crippled without God. They perish because they do not have any vision about life and its meaning and about the right way to find happiness. They need to know, they need to experience, that there is a God who loves them. They have to realise that their lives are only worthwhile if God becomes important to them.

The worst poverty today is the poverty of not having spiritual values in life. It is more crippling than material poverty. We Christians have to realise just how much we have to give, simply because we are baptized. Our solidarity with Christ is deepened each time we receive him in Holy Communion. We have within us a power to do wonderful things for God. We have the proud name of Christian; we are followers of Christ; we belong to him. Why is it then that we so often lack confidence? Why do we think we are helpless? In the meantime the city of man goes on its way hungry, and in a sense lost.

*   *   *

We live in a world where so much has been achieved. Our generation knows how to put men on the moon, but does not know the meaning of life. It looks to the people of faith for help. But often we remain silent, uncertain how to respond. We have to cure that lack of confidence. How do we do it? The answer is simple but very demanding. We need the inspiration of the Spirit; we need to speak about God as people who know Him, as people who have seen the invisible. It can only happen if we learn to pray. We must appreciate and understand the value of prayer in our lives; parishes must become schools of prayer; families should build their unity on prayer together; our lay organisations will only limp along unless they help their members to pray more intensely. Whenever we come together for meetings we should always spend some time praying together. I would not be happy if that meant only saying formal prayers together.

This country will become Christian again when groups of people come together and know that "where two or three are gathered together in his name, there he is in their midst". They will meet, perhaps just to share silence in the presence of God, or to pray aloud, helping one another. That should take place in every family every day. It should be introduced to every meeting or assembly of Christians. Then we would become sensitive to the will of God. We would be open to the guidance of the Holy Spirit.

*   *   *   *

Search for meaning

What lies deepest in the heart of man, in all that he does and in the manner of his thinking, is his striving to discover meaning, to escape from the absurd. The mind of man is in search of meaning, his heart is in search of happiness, a happiness which will be complete and unending. We are restless, as St Augustine says, until our hearts rest in Him who is truth and goodness, the explanation of all things, the true object of our loving.

*   *   *

That tension between whether we can know God or whether we cannot know Him was expressed by St Augustine when he said it is far better to love God than to know Him. It is difficult to love someone you do not know. But knowledge of God and love of God feed each other, as it were. If you try to love Him you come to know Him. As you get to know Him, you love Him more.

We talk of knowing *about* God, whereas the point is to know God. We want to know God, that is why there must be prayer in our lives. It is only in the experience of praying that we become aware not only that we seek God, but that God is always seeking us. That realisation can come in all sorts of ways. Often we come closest to Him when we experience weakness and suffering. God can speak to us when we are most desolate. Our search often begins when tragedy befalls us. We then begin to look.

We are slow to understand that God is searching for us, because we are deaf and blind. Our modern civilisation with its emphasis on scientific and technological achievement is in danger of making us less and less receptive to God, and so less inclined to listen and look. But when science and human skill fail us and we feel helpless and weak, that can be a golden moment. We are no longer self-sufficient.

*   *   *

Every individual searches for meaning in life, an explanation of existence and of life's experience. At the same time every individual searches for happiness, for that ecstasy which is to be found in its most intense form in the experience of love.

The search for meaning and happiness is, in point of fact, a single search. It seeks what lies above, beyond and outside oneself. It reaches out to grasp this reality, this transcendence, this Absolute, and - here is the deepest level of truth - this reality and transcendence is found to be a living God, a personal and infinite God.

We all experience this search and hunger to a greater or lesser extent. But this is our human way of describing and experiencing an even more intense search and hunger, God's search and hunger for us.

*   *   *   *   *

God looks for us

When adults play hide and seek with young children, the children can never lose. It would be a bad game if adults hid in some place where they could not be found. We make certain that we can be. If, by chance, the child still fails, then we go in search. Is there not something similar in God? He gives us any number of opportunities to find Him. And even if we become distracted and stop looking, He will take an initiative - a happy experience possibly, or one involving tragedy or sadness – and come looking for us. He wants us. Never doubt that. It is foolish to hide from Him.

* * *

I like the concept of man being in search of God. Slowly we come to realise that it is only one way of speaking of our response to God's search for us. That is where the initiative lies. God in search of man reveals Himself in a way which the created universe cannot. It is a special kind of revelation. It reached its high point when the Son of God became man.

* * * * *

Chinks in the cloud of unknowing

In searching for meaning and purpose in life, we are trying to catch glimpses of the glory of God.

We cannot look directly at the sun with a naked eye. The eye is too weak, the sun too strong. Our natural limitations are further hampered by weaknesses which stem from our human and inherited sinfulness.

It is as if a cloud hovered between us and God. From time to time that cloud of unknowing is pierced by a shaft of light which shows us something about God, though we do not see or touch Him directly.

It may be a moment of total happiness, an experience of true love, a discovery of another of the secrets locked away in the created universe. Conversely, it may be in sorrow and sadness that we experience His presence. In ecstasies and agonies, His voice is unmistakable to those who are prepared to listen and to look. Such shafts of light give warmth to the heart.

The author of the *Cloud of Unknowing* wrote: "The higher part of contemplation – at least as we know it in this life – is wholly caught up in darkness, and in this cloud of unknowing, with an outreaching love and a blind groping for the naked being of God, Himself and Him only" (ch. 8). And yet we have to "strike that thick cloud of unknowing with the sharp dart of longing love . . . " (ch. 6).

In love, the lover perceives in the beloved depths hitherto unknown. Often we see because we love. We understand and marvel, and love then grows. That human experience of love can help us to fashion that 'sharp dart of longing love' which will pierce the cloud and allow the warmth of God's love to come through to us. We have to discover the deeper meaning of all our human experience, for our experience can lead us to God and to catching a glimpse of His glory.

"Still, Lord, you hide from my soul in your light and beauty, and therefore it still lives in darkness and in misery", wrote St Anselm. "I look all round, but I do not see your beauty. I listen, but I do not gather your fragrance. I taste, but do not know your savour. I touch, but do not feel your yielding. For, Lord God, it is in your own unutterable manner that you have these things; you have given them to what you have created in a manner which can be felt, but the senses of my soul have been hardened, dulled, and blocked by the ancient sickness of sin" (Proslogion, ch. 17).

Our senses receive shafts of His glory in accordance with their different capacities: sight, taste, hearing. The eyes, ears and indeed taste and touch as well, are windows through which we receive shafts of the glory of God. Our minds must go beyond those sense experiences to think about the glory of God. Those experiences are ways of bringing that glory into our lives. It is much more so in the experience of loving; it is so, too, in our appreciation of beauty and our response to it.

*   *   *

There will be a moment when we shall see beauty in its purest form. It will be a moment of ecstasy. We shall wonder and admire, for its magnificence will delight and please. We shall have entered into the eternal 'now' of total fulfilment. We shall have seen Him as He is, that glory which at present is hidden from us by the cloud of unknowing.

The eye perceives proportion, shape and colour, all parts of that which we call beauty. The ear too knows sounds that please and delight. But the beauty which the eye beholds, or which pleases the ear, speaks of something other than itself; it speaks of God.

When we for our part strive to acknowledge what we believe Him to be, we use those things which are the most noble and best in God's creation and man's achievement. A thing of beauty speaks to us of the beauty of God. To praise His goodness and His majesty we communicate with Him in language which has dignity, with music that is noble and in buildings of distinction and merit.

There is a beauty which is the most pleasing to Him, more pleasing than the greatest music, more important than the finest architecture. We call it beauty of the heart, which is another way of speaking of the first of the eight Beatitudes: "Blessed are the poor in spirit for they shall see God". Purity of heart, the sense of dependence, the aching longing for God, the inner wounds that cry out for His healing hand, these cause us to turn to God. If we remain unassuming and little, if we recognise our weakness and need, we are ready for His coming. If we remain open to His life and ready to do His will we are guaranteed the full and lasting vision of Him.

In a great Cathedral like Westminster, it is right that we should use all that is fine and magnificent to give honour and glory to God. But as I write I remember a prison chaplain celebrating Mass in a shapeless room made clean and tidy for the occasion. It is no place of beauty and the congregation is composed of the wounded ones of our society; their musical talents minimal, their clothing drab and dull. But God is smiling on them as He does on the congregation of the Cathedral. They too are doing their best, and like the rest of us, are pleasing to God.

Our great Cathedral is home for all. It is here to serve the needs of all men and women, to help them on their journey through life. It is right that we should be a chink in the cloud of unknowing, enabling our parishioners and visitors to glimpse something of the beauty of God. It is a place too to come for refreshment and to purify the heart. It is a place where men and women meet Christ, and, in and through Him, gain strength and courage to take another step along the road to God.

The sinner

Sense of sin

The times in which we live demand, I believe, that we have a more vivid awareness of sin in the world. Whenever we harden our hearts to the needs of others, we sin. Whenever we pursue pleasure for its own sake to the detriment of others, we sin. Whenever we inflict sorrow or hardship on others, we sin. It is not unusual these days to come across people with an unformed or distorted conscience, or with a conscience relying primarily on instinct or personal preference rather than on a sober awareness of right and wrong and on an acknowledgment of God's law. Christians need to be truly sensitive to sin. We should live lives which are a renunciation of sin. For goodness to prevail in the world, intelligent and consistent effort is required from people of good will.

There is sin in the world, and we are sinners. We are right to meditate at length and in depth on the mercy of God and His love for us. That theme offers endless possibilities of feeding our minds and warming our hearts. Yet we should not be blinded to the reality of sin which is part of our unhappy world and part of our own lives. It is foolish and dangerous self-deception to point the finger at other people without taking note of our own sins.

We sin from frailty and from malice. There are of course those sins of weakness when we are overcome by passion and by our weaknesses. There are those calculated and deliberate decisions to do what is wrong for the sake of our own advantage or self-interest. But in some measure, all of us are burdened with sin.

Our Lord Jesus Christ suffered and died on the cross

because of sin – not just the treachery of Judas, not just
the mistaken obedience and sense of duty of the Roman
soldiers, not just the weakness of Peter and the other
apostles who ran away, but the sinfulness of the rebel-
lious and stiff-necked world, the sin of men and women
down the ages. So each of us in some way contributed to
the passion and death of Our Lord. There is a certain
solidarity in sin.

That is not a reason for becoming depressed or overcome with guilt feelings. There must be sorrow, of
course; there must be avowal of our sin, and expression
of our sorrow; there must be a putting right of what has
been wrong. In the Catholic Church those of us in grave
sin, and conscious of it, are called upon to go to the
sacrament of Reconciliation, to confession. But then we
turn immediately to new life and we strike out again
vigorously on our pilgrim way to God.

*   *   *   *   *

Conversion of heart

The genius of man has built up in our age an imposing
scientific and technological empire, but the sinfulness
of man has made him a slave in his own kingdom.
Harmony does not reign in the kingdom of man, for
man is in conflict with man and nation with nation.
These fundamental divisions are the product of sin, for
sin is separation: man is separated from God, and man
from man.

It is the heart of the individual that is divided and
needs to be healed and made whole. The primacy of the
rule of God in the heart of each person is the foundation upon which justice and peace among men will be
built. There must first be repentance, for there is sin in

the world and we are all sinners. Once there is repentance, reconciliation will follow. And so the words of the Lord, "the kingdom of God is at hand; repent and believe the Gospel" (Mk 1,15), speak to us today as urgently as they spoke to past ages. They are words which not only contain an admonition but also provide the essential starting-point for the process of healing ourselves and society and so of achieving unity and peace.

When an individual realises his personal sinfulness, it ought not to lead to depression or to a sense of hopelessness; instead it should lead to an act of humility before God. It is this which prompts the individual to seek from God what he cannot achieve for himself, namely that peace which comes from forgiveness and that oneness with God which is the foundation of true happiness. "A contrite and humble heart, O God, thou wilt not despise" (Ps 50,19) is the prayer of a person who is beginning to experience that change of heart, of which the Gospel speaks. It is a prayer full of hope, a starting-point for nations as well as for individuals. It is the first step in that search for God which is the ultimate purpose and joy of all individuals called by God to embark on that search. Yet at every stage the contradictions and the consequences of sin persist.

The fathers of the Second Vatican Council pondered the enigma of man in the Constitution on the Church in the Modern World - Gaudium et Spes. There they explained that unless God enters into our understanding of the purpose of each person, that person remains "an unanswered question" (GS n. 21). On the one hand, they said: "as a creature he finds himself limited in several ways . . . weak and sinful, he often does what he would prefer not to do, and fails to do what he would wish. He is divided against himself . . .". And yet, say the bishops, he is aware of having "unlimited aspirations and of having a call to a higher life" (GS n. 10). It is this call which is the reason for hope, both for individuals and for society.

At his most noble, man longs to escape from his sinfulness, but, finding himself powerless and lost, he allows himself to be found by his heavenly Father who sent His Son to seek that which was lost. The will of God that all should be saved is constant and the means to it are always available. Yet we have the frightening freedom to say 'yes' or to say 'no'. Much of our history can be written as a commentary on man's refusal to say 'yes' to God. In our own day, people are making the same mistake, for they are trying to build the city of man outside the kingdom of God, and are manifestly failing. We need to repent when repentance is due, to be reconciled to God and to each other. Then, with the restoration of faith in the Gospel of Jesus Christ we can set about the task of spreading the kingdom of God, and achieving that unity and peace for which many in our day are craving. The 'civilisation of love' – a phrase dear to Pope Paul VI – is the antithesis of a society where fear and hatred often abound.

The Holy Father constantly calls us these days to an authentic, deep spiritual renewal, a true conversion of heart.

This is hardly surprising since the very first words of Our Lord as he began his public ministry were: "Repent and believe the Gospel". That is the great cry which echoes down the ages and should ring in the ears of every genuine follower of Jesus Christ.

Repent, we are told, turn away from sin, do penance. Believe the Gospel, not as an ideology to talk about, not as an abstract system of values to be discussed among learned persons. We are urged to turn to God, to be reconciled with the Father and reconciled with each other. It is the constantly reiterated appeal of Christ through the Church, the meaning of the Holy Year which Pope John Paul II decided upon in order to celebrate the nineteen hundred and fiftieth anniversary of the Redemption.

We have no illusions about ourselves or about the world in which we live. We have to engage daily in the struggle against selfishness and sin within our very selves. That is a relentless warfare. But there is a wider battle to be fought. The whole of humanity suffers from a weakness, but there is in addition real, deliberate sin in our world. There is the sin of neglecting God and the sin of direct disobedience of His law. Such evils are even on occasion enshrined in our laws. There is terrible cruelty among men and women and a deep-rooted injustice which is sometimes built into structures of national and international society.

There is need for repentance, for conversion, for reconciliation. Conversion begins deep within ourselves, it involves radical change inside ourselves which then alters the way we relate to God and to fellow human beings. It is not a switch of sympathies, the adoption of a different set of ideas. It is the adoption of a set of values. It is a change of heart. It leads us to embrace wholeheartedly what the Gospel says and to love Him who says it. It inspires us to work tirelessly for a more just and humane world.

* * *

"Behold the man", Pilate said as he brought Jesus before the crowd, with the crown of thorns upon his head and his body already in shreds from the scourging. Is this what man is really like? For surely if God had become man, should we not be looking at the perfection of all that is human?

"We saw him without beauty, without majesty, no looks to attract our eyes" (Is 53,2). The State, which Pilate represented, and the religious leaders for whom Caiaphas spoke, had done their work. The truth about God, the truth about man – well, "what is truth?", Pilate asked. Let everyone decide for himself or herself, Pilate might have gone on to say. He did not, but *we* do.

It is better to get rid of this man, better that one man should die than that the whole nation should perish, said Caiaphas the high priest. He might disturb everything and everybody with his teaching about the poor,

about the victims of injustice. We must not disturb the
established order of things. Caiaphas would probably
have gone on in this vein. He did not, *we* do.

So they killed him. The secular power, Pilate, and the
religious leader, Caiaphas, could have stopped it. But
they did not.

The kingdom of God cannot easily be given shape
and substance in the city of man. The two have existed
down the centuries, often locked in conflict with each
other and, at other times, operating, almost, in two
different worlds, seeking independence of each other in
a separation of Church and State. At Calvary it looked
as if Caesar had vanquished God. But the tomb does not
represent the burying of all our hope. The eyes of faith
enable us to look beyond the figure of the crucified
Christ to see the image of the Risen Lord, transfigured,
radiant, kingly in appearance as he emerges from the
tomb.

Those eyes of faith enable us to see in our pagan and
secular world the striving of many good people to bring
the values of the kingdom of God into the city of man
so often cruel and unthinking. Those eyes of faith can
also see in the agony of the world the possibility of
achieving God's purpose which is in the best interests of
man. Christ's acceptance of suffering brings the world
its peace. Through his wounds we are healed. There is a
healing to be given; there is a peace to be established.
It needs a change of heart and the will to act. That is
why the kingdom of God is so slow in coming. That is
why it is established first in the hearts and lives of
believers and continues to act as a leaven or as a mustard
seed in society. That is why we must pray, and ask
God's guidance and protection for a great many people
in positions of power and influence, and for the conversion of many. We have to turn the vision which was
Christ's into at least partial reality in our situation and
in our own time.

The redemption of man through Christ's death is
good news and very contemporary. It is we who have
grown cold. A world without God, a world, that is,

which runs as if God were not, has been tried all too often in history and always, as we have learnt to our cost today, has been found wanting. We should put our faith in Christ who died and rose again for us. That is the truly radical alternative for society today.

The new world, prophesied by Christ, is only possible if men and women are made new. If people change, the world changes. The kingdom of God continues to grow within the city of man.

It is never easy to escape from the darkness and harder still to attempt to be good. I do not mean 'good' exclusively, or even primarily, in a moral sense. I mean something more profound. It is what the Gospel calls a change of heart, in Greek 'metanoia'. It is something very radical undertaken by the individual which must, in the end, have a profound effect on the society in which he finds himself. It consists, in part, in the discovery that what we experience in our present state on this earth is not, and cannot be, the whole story. There is a reality about which science cannot speak and which technology cannot achieve. We enter the realm of the eternal, the spiritual, that is of religion.

* * * * *

The mercy and love of God

There are some words in the first eucharistic prayer of the Mass which always fill me with great joy and peace. We pray: "Though we are sinners, we trust in your mercy and love". It is good to be able to acknowledge honestly and humbly that we are sinners.

In the story of the pharisee and the publican at prayer in the synagogue, the publican, so conscious of his sinfulness, could only pray: "God, be merciful to me a sinner". That prayer, in my view, is one of the few prayers we can pray with total sincerity. Happily, as we know from Our Lord's words, that man was justified and saved. Because in his weakness, in his wretchedness, fully acknowledged and humbly confessed, he went straight to the heart of Our Blessed Lord.

God's love is manifested in Jesus Christ. It is a love which is merciful, that is, one that understands the weakness of man. His understanding and love are such that His will is to save. It is precisely because we are sinners, weak and guilty, that we need to be saved from ourselves, from the danger of failing to love Him, and to love each other. The greater the weakness and the graver the danger, the more overwhelming and tender is the love and concern of God for us in Jesus Christ.

The honest and humble acceptance of our frailty liberates us from pretence, from the effort of seeking to impress others and to justify ourselves. We can be truthful with ourselves and with others. We can welcome into our lives the saving and healing power of Christ. We have no other saviour. We need no other cure.

*　*　*　*　*

Forgiveness

When the pharisees criticised Our Lord for mixing with sinners, he uttered those words which are, to my mind at any rate, among the most precious and most comforting of all: "It is not those who are in health who have need of the physician, it is those who are sick" (Mt 9,12). Weakness, moral sickness and our crying need of salvation are not barriers between ourselves and God. They provide bonds which unite us to Him. Perfect love casts out fear, as St Paul says. In the spiritual lives of many persons fear dominates and not love. A spiritual life built on fear is built on the wrong foundations. Ultimately it is not pleasing to God and can never lead us to Him.

* * * * *

Reconciliation

The most powerful reason to bring us to repent, to be reconciled with God and with each other, is the thought of the Father's love for us. It is the certain knowledge that He is ever willing to forgive. The prophet Isaiah expresses movingly God's attitude to us: "Can a woman forget her child so as not to have pity on the son of her womb? Even if she should forget, yet I will not forget you" (Is 49,15).

We must not trifle with God, nor play Him false. But if we continue to make an effort, if we long for Him and want to find Him, He is there with His love to forgive, and to give us the riches that His Son won for us. For God is rich in mercy, and through Jesus Christ we, who are now members of the family of God, have been so richly blessed. The love of God for us and his abiding forgiveness can prove an irresistible attraction for those who become conscious of them. The barriers we try to erect crumble. We are drawn to God with increasing boldness when we learn of His love.

Because of the death and Resurrection of Our Lord Jesus Christ we are enabled to make that journey from sinfulness to life, hidden with Christ in God. The Gospel calls us to conversion of heart, to change, to become different.

Turning from what separates us from God demands that we say 'no'; 'no' to sin, 'no' to bad habits, 'no'

to being apathetic in our service of God and our neighbour, 'no' to all that disfigures us as human beings,
'no' to all that is displeasing to God. This 'no' to ourselves is self-denial. We need to put into practice in a
sensible and prudent manner some exercise of self-
denial in order to be better able to say 'no' to ourselves when our faults, weaknesses and sins are coming
between us and our love and service of God.

What is even more important is that we should say
'yes' to God: 'yes' to the demands He makes upon us,
'yes' to the suffering He might ask us to bear, 'yes' to
the love which He wants us to give.

Essential to our conversion is an increase in our life
of prayer, especially in our devotion to the Mass. If
we do this, then we can be certain that God will speak
to us and guide us. He will make increasingly clear to
us what in our lives prevents our having union with
Him. He wants that union, and, deep down, so do we.

From sin to union with God

From sin to union with God, that is the journey which each one of us has to travel; it is our human pilgrimage. Day by day we have to travel along that road, from that which separates us from God to that which unites us to Him.

*   *   *   *   *

Spiritual health

The doctor's experience of people, and the priest's, tell us that many are still bewildered, indeed haunted, by the perennial problems of pain, suffering and death. Anguish in the heart, fear of dying, an inner emptiness, a piercing loneliness, these are to be found in the secular society, a society from which God has been banished as unnecessary, unhelpful or even harmful; or one in which He is kept for Sunday and for private reflection only.

Secular society has not managed to resolve the really deep problems. We still fear and wonder about death; we dread suffering. The consumer society – the society in which we are offered every kind of material good and prosperity – has not satisfied the deepest longings of the human heart or given the joy and contentment for which every heart craves. Jung in his book *Modern Man in Search of a Soul* wrote:

". . . Among all my patients in the second half of life, there
has not been one whose problem in the last resort was not
that of finding a religious outlook on life. It is safe to say that
every one of them fell ill because he had lost that which the
living religions of every age have given their followers, and
none of them has been really healed who did not regain his
religious outlook".

I have often thought about that, and it has led me to
reflect that what is true for the individual is surely true
also for the individual in his or her relationship with
others, therefore in society itself. The patient may have
much wrong with him, but he can be cured. There are
always signs of hope, always good things to note.
Indeed, whatever the signs to the contrary, there remains
in each one of us at least a spark of religion to be
ignited into something brighter and warmer. The promise of a healing process is there.

How do we detect this spark within us? I imagine that
it is different in each person, which would not be surprising since every person is unique. I think it has something to do with a longing deep down within us. We long
to know and possess the good, or the good that we see
in a great number of persons and objects which fall
within our experience. In the end we discover that the
pursuit of truth and goodness leads us to long for truth
and goodness in their absolute form. This absolute truth
and this absolute goodness we call God.

There are threats to life and the quality of life.
Individuals and society cannot be fundamentally healed
without a radical transformation. Religion is essential
to this process. Personal renewal and renewal of society
follow the same pattern. A return to God is a pre-
condition for a return to health.

*   *   *   *   *

Humility

St Benedict has sometimes been called the master of humility, and his Rule became, and has always been, a classic on humility. For him the key to having the right spiritual attitudes is humility.

Humility is central to the Christian life; it is fundamental. It is a virtue which fits one to be a religious person. It is a virtue not only for monastic life, but for all Christian life.

Humility is not modesty, though modesty is one of its signs. It includes having a low opinion of oneself; it is facing the truth about who God is, and the truth of who I am.

Humility in another is a very beautiful thing to see; but the attempt to become humble is painful indeed. It hurts. It hurts to be criticised, to be misunderstood, to be misjudged, to be snubbed, to be written off; but such things are the high road to humility. None of us enjoys walking that way. Oddly enough, I believe that for some of us it is when we realise how little we are regarded by others that we begin to recognise how highly we are esteemed by God. We have ceased to wonder what others think about us; we have discovered our worth in the eyes of our Father.

* * *

It is my experience that men and women of true eminence and real wisdom often have a deep humility. They know their own limitations and how much they do not know. It is good to meet a very learned but wise person, and to find in that person the wonder and simplicity of a child.

The wise men who came from the East were learned, and men of high position. But their wisdom and their learning enabled them to stoop and be small in the presence of a Child whom they recognised to be greater

than they. They had humility; that is why they knelt
and gave their gifts; their gifts expressed their humility.

* * *

At some time in our lives, we may feel that we are
failures. We have experienced great disappointments,
and the sense of being less good than we should be, of
being less successful than we would like to be. This
sense of failure and inadequacy is common among
us. Our Lord must have felt like this at the end of his
life. Everybody had turned against him. They were
going to execute him; they were insulting him. We
know that this moment of failure was God's moment
of success. That is a most important fact to learn.
Whenever I feel inadequate or a failure, disappointed
or upset, God can enter into my life, and bring His
success.

* * * *

Crocks and crooks

Many people simply cannot face up to the demands
of the Gospel, either because the ideal seems far beyond
them, or becuase they live in circumstances and situations which make it impossible for them to do much
more than just survive each day with the vague hope
that at the end of their lives things will somehow work
out. For example, a person may be caught up in a marriage situation unrecognised by the Church but from
which, for all kinds of reasons, there seems no escape.
The demands of God upon us are very great. Sin, the
deliberate violation of God's law, can never be con-
doned or accepted. Is there, then, no hope for most of
us, men and women who simply cannot aspire to holiness? And what of those of us who have tried so often
and so hard to overcome bad habits or to break with sin

and yet have so dismally failed? Is God uninterested in us? Will He reject us? That is a frightening question. The answer is, I trust, clear and certain. He never rejects us; it is we who are free to reject Him. Some do. But, happily, many of us struggle on, starting all over again but failing all too often. We are the weak and wounded ones, failures certainly in our eyes. But are we necessarily failures in God's eyes? How does He regard us, our struggles and failures? It is when we look at the gospels and meditate on Our Lord's own words and on his actions that we shall find the answers to these questions.

Let us look again at the story of the publican and the pharisee, as recorded for us by St Luke (Lk 18,9–14): "There were some who trusted in themselves as just, and despised others. . . ". The story starts with a warning. They thought they had found acceptance with God and, clearly, had not. Equally clearly they did not realise it. Indeed the pharisee in the story had every reason to believe that he was well regarded by God: "I fast twice in a week, I give tithes of all I possess", and he had no record of theft, cheating or adultery. Here was a man who practised his religion meticulously, and morally speaking had an admirable record. But he had a fatal flaw. Like others of his kind he "despised the rest of the world" and he looked down on the poor tax-collector upon whom he sat in judgment and whom he condemned. There is nothing more dangerous, nor more hideous, than spiritual pride. It is a very subtle thing, and it can all too easily creep into our lives. When we despise others, think we are superior, feel satisfied with our spiritual effort – these are manifestations of spiritual pride.

All this is very much opposed to the attitude of the tax-collector. He had nothing to boast about. He just "stood some distance away, not daring even to raise his eyes to heaven". He could only beat his breast and say: "God, be merciful to me a sinner". I cannot think of any prayer which we can so easily make our own. However burdened we may be by our past sins, or by our present difficulties, however much we may feel ourselves to be failures, and failures in God's eyes, we can always pray: "God, be merciful to me a sinner". You will remember the comment made by Our Lord about the tax-collector's prayer: "I tell you, this man went down into his house justified rather than the other; because everyone that exalts himself shall be humbled, and he that humbles himself shall be exalted" (ibid v. 14). The tax-collector hated his sin. His prayer for forgiveness included the will to try to overcome his sinfulness.

We must not, of course, condone sin; we must not be complacent about our weakness. But it is good to recognise that we are weak and wounded and to identify with that tax-collector. Perhaps we need to go on failing so as to become truly humble, to recognise at last that whatever is good and right in us comes as a gift from God. It is our part to try not to sin, to try to please God in all things. We go on trying. That is a gift from God. Our success is also a gift from God, given to one who wants to receive it.

Our Lord often met sick people and sinners, crocks and crooks. A prayerful study of how he handled them tells us much about the way God looks upon us in our weakness. We are also presented with a number of prayers which we can make our own. Take, for instance, the account of the curing of the leper in St Mark's gospel (Mk 1,40–45). The leper is you and I. His physical wounds and weaknesses are the mirror in which we can see our spiritual problems and difficulties; his prayer can be our prayer. The leper prayed: "If it be thy will, thou hast power to make me clean". We are then told that Our Lord "was moved with pity". I like to reflect on Our Lord looking at me as I struggle to be what I know I should be, and fail; as I try to love both him and my neighbour, and get it wrong. But he knows that I want to try and that, surely, moves him to pity me. He may cure me instantly, as he did the leper: "It is my will, be thou made clean" (v. 41). On the other hand he may want us to go on trying to be better or more committed Christians, and leave us for a time with our wounds and weaknesses. Perhaps, however, he can only heal us slowly and over the years. One thing is certain: he does listen and he does answer but in his way and as he thinks is best for us. It is also certain that we are often not aware of the moment or timing of his healing hand upon our wounds. We have to trust him.

There are, as I have said, so many encounters of Our Lord with either the 'crooks' or the 'crocks'. In each case the contact and the dialogue can become a conversation between Our Lord and ourselves. For example, that "blind man sitting by the wayside begging" (Lk 18,35–43) is, as in the case of the leper, an image of you or me as we make our pilgrim way through life. We are like blind people. We do not see God. We often do not see clearly the way ahead, either for ourselves or others. We are bewildered and helpless; so we pray as the blind man prayed: "Jesus, son of David, have pity on me". We may well be tempted to think that turning to Our Lord is a waste of time. All kinds of reasons will crowd into our minds to dissuade us. ("I've tried it before and nothing happened".) St Luke tells us that the blind man was told to be quiet – "they rebuked him and told him to be silent". He was not put off. He cried out all the more, "Son of David, have pity on me". Then Our Lord intervened and ordered the man to be brought to him. "What wouldst thou have me do for thee?" he asked. That question is addressed to us. God speaks to each one and asks, "What can I do for you?" And we pray: "Lord, give me back my sight, just let me see". Is that prayer always answered? The answer is 'yes', but always in God's way and not necessarily in ours.

God has only one over-riding desire for us, and that is union with Him. How He brings that about is very often hidden from us. Sometimes He gives sufficient sight to see the next step, quite often no more than enough power to the inner eye to pick out the person who will lead and guide us. That person is Jesus Christ. We remain weak and wounded, and we go on praying for that extra help and strength to keep going. The result is not dramatic, but enough for us to rejoice and glorify

God who has given us what He thinks we need. It is no bad thing to remain a 'crock' and in need of constant help. "They that are in health need not a physician, but they that are ill" (Mt 9, 12). He has come for us. If you love a person, you want to help. To the end of our lives most of us need that help – badly; and He wants to give it – very much.

*   *   *   *   *

Be not afraid

"Why should I rejoice?" you might say. It is my life's experience that there is no day on which I shall keep from tears and not know sadness or misfortune. I weep bitter tears for myself when my mind knows only anguish and anxiety, my body pain and fatigue. If God be the goodness which is claimed for Him, if He has that love for us which no human love can match, then why does evil seem to rule our hearts and hold sway in His creation? Yet His message is still: "Rejoice, do not be afraid".

Terror comes when we see no escape from the darkness that surrounds us, when we see no light. Terror is the child of despair, ugly and cruel. But when terror holds us in its grip, hope is often born. Darkness yields to light. A Saviour has been born, the Lord Christ himself, for "God so loved the world as to give His only begotten Son; that whosoever believeth in him may not perish, but may have life everlasting" (Jn 3,16).

Do not be afraid. We need never be alone. Every burden carried by us is also shared by him. "Give me your burden", he says, "and I will make it mine". He will not always lift the burden from us, but being his, too, it is lighter now and easier.

We do not understand why we are fallen and sinful, burdened and wounded. He does not will our sadnesses or our pain. He wants us to know his goodness and to trust, to find his love and rejoice. The secret hidden in his words will slowly be shown us. It is the secret of his love, warm, close and true. That love is the meaning of his life; it is the reason of his mission when he came to us as man.

SECTION TWO
God the Pilgrim

God in search of us

If you ever feel depressed or downcast, or if you are tempted to give up the practice of your Faith, then go and find some quiet place, take with you a New Testament, turn to the fifteenth chapter of St Luke's gospel and read it slowly and prayerfully.

There are three stories told by Our Lord himself. They are addressed to you personally by him. Each of the stories speaks about something that was lost: a coin, a sheep, and, the most important of the three, a son. In all three cases there is a search on the part of the person who has lost the precious object. A woman sweeps out the house frantically; the shepherd leaves the other ninety-nine sheep; and the father waits – for he can do no other – for his prodigal son to return. Each day the father goes out just in case he might see his son coming home again. He waits and hopes, anxiously. Then one day he sees him. "While he was still a long way off, his father saw him and took pity on him: running up he threw his arms round his neck and kissed him" (v. 20). That is no ordinary account of a father greeting a wayward son. We are concerned here with the Word of God, with one of the clearest revelations of the truth of God's love of us. He is always present, waiting for us to turn to Him. When we do He is there to embrace us and to shower us with His gifts. Could you ever doubt God's love for you after reading and meditating on that passage? No wonder an experienced mystic could write:

> "The love of God most high for our soul is so wonderful that it surpasses all knowledge. No created being can know the greatness, the sweetness, the tenderness of the love that our Master has for us. By His grace and help therefore let

us in spirit stand and gaze, eternally marvelling at the supreme, single-minded, surpassing, incalculable love that God, who is goodness, has for us. Then we can ask reverently of our lover whatever we will. For by nature our will wants God and the good-will of God wants us. We shall never cease wanting and longing until we possess Him in fulness and joy. Then we shall have no further wants. Meanwhile His will is that we go on knowing and loving until we are perfected in heaven" (Julian of Norwich: *Revelations of Divine Love*, ch. 6, Edition Clifton Wolters).

The mercy of the Father is strong. That mercy is both tenderness and fidelity to those He has created for union with Him. Tenderness and steadfastness are a powerful combination, and they are the reason for God wanting to be involved closely with us. It is thus that I understand those words of St John: "God so loved the world that He gave up His only begotten Son, that whosoever believeth in Him may not perish, but may have life everlasting" (Jn 3,16). Because He so loved us, He became, in His Son Jesus Christ, a pilgrim like us.

*   *   *   *   *

The mystery of the Incarnation

The Christian Church is not the product of human wisdom. It is not primarily motivated by humanitarian concern. It is the guardian and herald of a revelation from God, and so it deals in mysteries. Mysteries are profound truths beyond the grasp of our unaided intellects, yet yielding their riches to the humble and prayerful.

The account of the creation in the Book of Genesis contains a wealth of meaning. God, for the Jew and the Christian, is no impersonal force. He is the creator acting with intelligence and love. From the beginning, human beings are pictured as altogether special, set apart from the rest of creation – "Man made in the image of God" – not because they are flesh and blood but because they have within themselves a divine spark, the power of reasoning, the capacity to choose and love. Each individual reflects something of God, and was destined by God to be a familiar friend, walking together with Him among the delights of paradise.

But pride, self will, disobedience shattered the innocence of the Garden of Eden. Man made by God and for God, rebelled against God, and entered a world of conflict and sin. At war within himself, in conflict with his neighbours, he defied God and plunged the world into darkness.

The whole of the Bible tells the story of how God went in search of man, of how the Good Shepherd restored the scattered flock to the sheepfold, of how the Creator refashioned that image of Himself, for so long disfigured by men, for so long broken into fragments by sin. He remade man in the person of Jesus Christ, offering mankind a new life, a more glorious destiny, a new image of itself, a new model.

In Jesus Christ, the believer perceives a twofold reality. The eyes of faith gaze on him and see what man can be, and is meant by God to be. At the same time, the believer can trace in the features of Jesus the image of God the Father. Philip said: "Lord, show us the Father, and it is enough for us". Jesus answered: "Have I been so long a time with you and have you not known me? Philip, he that seeth me seeth the Father also. How sayest thou, 'Show us the Father'? Do you not believe that I am in the Father and the Father in me?" (Jn 14,8–10).

This surely is where Christianity stands alone. Central to our faith is the belief that God became man. In Jesus Christ we stand at the point of intersection between the divine and the human. In Christ we see what God offers to humanity, and what humanity can grasp of the divine.

*   *   *   *   *

Faith in the Incarnation

No man can say "God became man" unless it is the
Spirit within him who prompts that act of faith. So
when we celebrate a great feast our attitude must
always be one of helpless humility, recognising that it
is never by any power of our own that we can take one
step of progress in our understanding of the things of
God. It is a gift, and one for which we must ask earnestly, sincerely and constantly.

If we do not believe, we remain in the dark and the
dark brings fear and sadness. If we do not believe, we
miss the true meaning of life and the future has no hope.

How, for example, do we see our celebration each
Christmastide? What is our belief? Do we go the whole
way and kneel at the crib and say, "Yes, God became
man in Jesus Christ"? For it is that which we celebrate
on Christmas night; that and nothing less. To believe in
the fact that God became man is not to walk in doubt
and illusion, it is to step into the world of God and so
into reality. The entry of God Himself into our world is
the occasion and the means by which we enter into
God's own world.

Without that firm belief in the Incarnation there can
never be true peace, true joy, true hope and good-will
among people. Perhaps one of the great difficulties of
our modern age, and for many Christians too, is that we
only half believe, half doubt. We do not go the whole
way and say "I believe" with total conviction.

The act of faith, our ability to make it, is a gift from
God for which we have to ask, and it demands a humility
of mind which is not a characteristic of contemporary
man.

*   *   *

The Christmas celebration, like all great feasts of the
Church, is a celebration of the mystery of God's love

for us. It is often easier to understand the love we have for others in our hearts; it is less easy to understand, or guess at, the love which others have for us. That is true about human love; it is even more true when we come to think and talk about the love of God. God so loved the world that He sent us His only begotten Son. That is a familiar truth which contains mystery. It is made richer still by the fact that God who became man was prepared to lay down his life for us. No greater love has any man than the love which prompts him to lay down his life for his friends. But what of the love that will die for the worthless, the enemy? The characteristics of Christian love are: to dedicate ourselves to others, to be totally available to others, to put the interests of others before our own. Christ Our Lord lived that kind of love to the utmost limit. He showed us what God should mean to us, and what we mean to God.

* * *

When God became man, humanity's view of God had to be completely recast. We cannot now have a concept of God which does not take into account how the divine has been translated into the human in the person of Jesus Christ. Nor can we fully understand man, and what man should be, unless we study Christ. Man is re-made in the image and likeness of Christ; Christ is the image and likeness of God the Father.

In the encyclical *Redemptor Hominis* Pope John Paul II wrote: "In man's history, the revelation of God's love and mercy has taken the name and form of Jesus Christ". Jesus Christ is God's love and mercy become incarnate.

Central to our faith in Jesus Christ, true God and true man, is what he did for us by dying on the Cross and rising again to life. It is difficult to understand the great mystery of love which we call the redemption. It is a real secret, hard to grasp, and then only by the help of the Holy Spirit.

*   *   *

We come closest to that mystery of the redemption when we offer the Sacrifice of the Mass, making the offering of ourselves in union with the supreme and eternal offering of Christ in love and obedience on Calvary. In Holy Communion we are united with Christ and absorbed by him in his self-giving. We become part of the whole Christ, the body of Christ, offered to the Father at each Mass – that is our pledge which has to be honoured in every decision we subsequently make throughout our daily lives. We do all, experience all, in union with our crucified and risen Lord.

*   *   *   *   *

Thoughts on Christ's Sacrifice

When a much loved relative, or close friend, dies, the memory of that loved one lingers in our minds. Time and again we like to think about that person. We like to remember the little things which seemed so characteristic of him or her; a certain look, physical mannerisms, special reactions. We begin to remember words and things said to us. We remember signs of affection, especially any indication that we were important to that loved one. Then a certain sadness mingles in our thoughts as we recall the last moments, the last hours, and we treasure especially the last words, the final message. We find all that to be very important, and we look around for something to remind us of the loved one, cherished memories made vivid by this or that object. Then we rummage round for letters, and they speak often after death with a poignancy and a directness which may have eluded us in life.

That kind of experience is one surely known to most of us, and it is that experience which the Church lives in those days which we call Holy Week; the loved one is Our Lord Jesus Christ. We go over and over in our song, in our prayer, in the liturgy generally, the important events and his last words.

On the Thursday of Holy Week we recall the time when Our Lord at the Last Supper got up and washed the feet of his disciples, and showed us something of the divine courtesy, for Our Lord reveals what is divine. He washed the feet of his disciples to show the regard which God has for us. That in itself is an astonishing thought. If such is the courtesy of God towards us, what in return can we show to Him? And with what respect and sensitivity should we treat our families, friends and acquaintances?

On Maundy Thursday we recall that first occasion when he took bread and changed it into his Body, when he took wine and changed it into his Blood. That truth requires from us faith, which is his gift. We need humility of mind to acknowledge that what was once bread is now his Body, what was once wine is now his Blood. Our act of faith in that great truth needs to be renewed constantly and to grow. We grow to recognise that in the Mass we have the means given by him to us to be taken up into his passion, death and Resurrection. Every Mass is a celebration both of Good Friday and Easter Sunday. Maundy Thursday was the day on which these two realities, his death and Resurrection, were made accessible to us in sign and sacrament in the Mass. The Mass is both Sacrifice and Banquet. It is central to the life of the Church. It gives value and meaning to our daily lives, to our loves, our pain, our endeavours. Every Maundy Thursday is a time to thank God for the Mass, for the daily miracle which makes sense of life.

After the ceremony is completed we prepare for Good Friday in prayerful mood, slipping perhaps into a church to pray at the chapel of repose. When close to him in the Blessed Sacrament we are close to him as he suffered in the Garden of Gethsemane, close to him as

Mary Magdalene was, when she met him in the garden on the first Easter Sunday.

* * * * *

The Garden of Gethsemane

In the Garden of Gethsemane Our Lord became sad. He was plunged into the deepest distress and sorrow. He was lonely, fearful. Whenever we hear of someone in distress we normally feel sorry for them and want to go and help them, by sharing in some way their sorrow. Very often the only possible thing is just to be with them. When people are suffering terrible pain, it can be irritating to say too much. We just share it with them, silently and lovingly. That is what we must do in our prayer, contemplating Christ's suffering, aware of the pain that still transfixes the heart of the world.

"My soul is sad, to the point of death". After they had finished the supper, Jesus went out to the garden to pray. Sick at heart, apprehensive, he did not want to be alone. "Would you, Peter, James and John, watch with me?" They had been together on another very different occasion, a triumphant one, when he had been transfigured before their very eyes. Then he had seemed more than human. But now he was sick at heart. Judas had gone to do his worst. The others? They would soon run away. The three companions sought in sleep the peace they could not find awake.

It is easy enough to describe the inflicting of physical pain. It is very difficult to describe what can go on in the depth of another's soul. The suffering which cannot be described is usually more intense than the suffering which is apparent to all. That sadness of soul cost Jesus so much in his agony in the garden that the sweat on his brow was like blood (cf. Lk 22,44). That is an image that has moved Christians down the ages, but the sadness in his soul cannot be described. There is a depth of sadness here which can never be shared by another person, never eased. It can only be glimpsed by one who loves deeply.

There is an added difficulty in appreciating the suffering experienced by Christ. Christ is God. It is true to say that God, in Our Lord, at that point, was troubled in spirit. It tells us something about God. Is there in God wounded love? Is there in God this feeling of being rejected, being turned down? We can only ask the question. We are already talking about something we could not possibly understand. But is there not something important here that Our Lord wanted us to glimpse? We can reject God; we can refuse His love; some of us can even treat God as Judas treated Our Lord. That is a frightening thought, because Our Lord pined for the love of Judas. God too pines for our love.

These are deep thoughts. We should think about Our Lord's suffering and what it means for us, and how his suffering can tell us something about God. But it can also be a great help to us in another way. We all suffer, sometimes in small ways, sometimes in great. Sometimes we have to live with great worries and at others endure terrible tragedies. Sometimes we are troubled in spirit, dismayed or full of sadness. In times of suffering we remember what happened to Our Lord and we can reach out to him for strength, understanding and sympathy. The Man of Sorrows has already offered to the Father the pain we now experience. It helped to fill the chalice he accepted in Gethsemane.

When we suffer and are sad, we are sharing then in Our Lord's passion; we are close to him and he is close to us. He leads us through his passion, to something much better and much greater, to a new life with a fresh hope. That is the meaning of the Resurrection.

*   *   *   *   *

Good Friday

"No greater love hath a man than he lay down his life for his friends". In the death of Christ, God made man, God's love for us is demonstrated and proclaimed with a power and intensity that will always overwhelm the humble and believing heart.

There is great suffering in the world, and death is the common destiny of every individual. By accepting them and sharing them, Our Lord has given suffering and death their own dignity. When I suffer, I am like Our Lord in the garden or carrying that heavy load on the way to Calvary. When I die, what happens to me is what he endured. That will be my consolation one day.

It was man's sin that made Our Lord suffer and which killed him. In a vivid and frightening way, we see in the passion what it means to reject God wilfully and deliberately; we glimpse something of the horror of sin and the wonder of God's love. Mankind has sinned and created a world in its own image and likeness. It became a world of pride, hatred and aggression; man became the prey of man. The love and healing of God came into that world in the person of Jesus Christ and was rejected. Darkness and evil struggled with light and goodness. Christ remained constant in love and accepted the will of his Father to the bitter end. On Calvary the power of this world seemed to have triumphed, but in defeat there was victory, in death there was life. To this day, the struggle continues. In our pain and suffering and striving Christ dies yet lives.

We pray, on Good Friday, for all mankind. Christ died for all men; each is precious to him. That is why the whole Christian community is concerned for all men and prays for them in the great intercessions of that day's liturgy. After those prayers, we come to the altar to venerate the Cross. It is a very personal and individual action. Our forefathers called it "creeping to the Cross". I like the expression. Each of us carries quietly and silently his or her own burden, a private sorrow, a secret pain, a personal grief. We creep with our load to the Cross. The simple gesture of kissing the wounds of Christ helps to heal the wounds we carry within ourselves.

To share suffering with another can sometimes, but not always, lighten the burden. To share it with Our Lord is altogether different. It is a moment of grace. It never fails.

When we venerate the Cross we think of those who are themselves nailed upon it every day by the cruelty and callousness of their fellow men, and think of Christ suffering again in them: the victims of war, the starving and destitute, the prisoners of conscience, the rejects and outcasts of our acquisitive society.

We look beyond the Cross and behind the tortured figure, and we can see dimly outlined, with the eyes of faith, the face of the risen Christ.

*   *   *   *   *

The Seven Last Words

The last words of a dying person are precious indeed, and they are all the more so when that person is a cherished member of the family, one greatly loved and much respected. What is he trying to say? What is it that he is trying to convey, and what is the meaning of it? Sometimes, it will be a word that speaks of his suffering and pain. At other times, it will be a word of comfort, a last message to console, something to be remembered and treasured. So the early Church remembered the last words of Jesus Christ, the ones he spoke as life ebbed away from him. The early Christians pondered on them, dwelt upon them, and down the ages men and women have sought, in their reflections and prayers, to find their deeper meaning. The early Christians had slowly begun to realise that this Jesus, whom they had known, was in fact the Christ, the Messiah, the anointed one, for whom they had waited so long and whom they so earnestly desired. But they came to see even more. This man, Jesus, the Messiah, was indeed truly God. That was a truth their minds could scarcely grasp. It was harder still when they had seen him so humiliated and so cruelly put to death. They had hoped for so much. It seemed to have ended in tragedy.

That sense of tragedy did not last, for the news that the tomb was empty, and the realisation that death itself had not kept him captive, filled them with joy and gave them new hope.

The gospels recorded the incidents of his life, the things which he said and did. This was to instruct his followers and those who were to come after him, you and I among them. They wrote at length about his passion and death, for this had great significance for them. And they recorded his last words, the seven last words. These were not just the words of a dying man; they were more. The human voice of the dying Christ was speaking to them of divine thoughts and attitudes, and as he died, amid terrible suffering, these words were, not only deeply moving and poignant, but very solemn. Each of these 'last words' has the power to transform lives for they are the Word of God. It is not possible to realise at once all the riches they contain. They reveal their secrets, slowly, if we meditate on them and pray.

We read in the gospels:

Lk 23,33f   *And when they reached the place which is named after a skull, they crucified him there . . . Jesus meanwhile was saying, "Father forgive them; they know not what they do". And they divided his garments among themselves by lot . . .*

Lk 23,39–43   *And one of the two thieves who hung there fell to blaspheming against him . . . But the other . . . said to Jesus, "Lord remember me when thou comest into thy Kingdom". And Jesus said to him, "I promise thee, this day thou shalt be with me in Paradise".*

Jn 19,25   *Meanwhile his mother . . . had taken her stand beside the Cross of Jesus. And Jesus, seeing his mother there, and the disciple, too, whom he loved, standing by, said to his mother, "Woman, this is thy son". Then he said to his disciple, "this is thy mother". And from that hour the disciple took her into his own keeping.*

Mt 27,45   *From the sixth hour onwards there was darkness over all the earth until the ninth hour; and about the ninth hour Jesus cried out in a loud voice, "My God, my God, why hast thou forsaken me?"*

Jn 19,28–30   *And now Jesus knew well that all was achieved which the Scripture demanded for its accomplishment; and he said, "I thirst". There was a jar there full of vinegar; so they filled a sponge with the vinegar and put it on a stick of hyssop, and brought it close to his mouth. Jesus drank the vinegar and said, "It is achieved".*

Lk 23,46   *And Jesus said, crying with a loud voice, "Father, into thy hands I commend my spirit", and yielded up his spirit as he said it.*

First Word

"Father, forgive them; they know not what they do"

"They know not what they do". They had scourged
him, lacerating his body; they had put a crown of thorns
on his head; they had insulted him, made fun of him.
They were now nailing him to the cross. And yet
in what they were doing the Roman soldiers were
degrading themselves more than him. "They know not
what they do" – surely their very humanity should
have prevented them from inflicting upon another
what they could not have faced themselves. That man
should be so cruel to man – it was so then and it is
often so in our own time, man's inhumanity to man.
"We know not what we do" – that word is profound.
The human voice of the Lord in his agony shows forth,
here, a divine generosity which is surprising, and so very
consoling. It is as if the Lord wants to go further than
we could ever go to excuse us. He will find any reason
to relieve us of the burden of guilt, if he can. Indeed the
Roman soldiers knew no better. Their training had made
them ruthless and very cruel. Of course, their actions
are to be condemned: someone must be responsible and
so be guilty, but these men . . . "they know not what
they do". So he prays: "Father, forgive them . . . ".
Were there ever words so sweet to the ears of those burdened and weighed down by wrong-doing and sin? In
every human life there are things, actions and attitudes
that need forgiveness; there are memories of foolishness and weakness, that lurk like dark spectres to haunt
us when the spirit is low or the going hard. If only we
could hear, clearly and within us, that we have been
forgiven. The Roman soldiers had not asked for forgiveness, and yet he had asked that it should be given to
them. If you and I truly want forgiveness, if our sorrow
is real, what is it that stops us from knowing that we
have been forgiven? Is it our failure to believe in His
love for us? He loved those Roman soldiers, though
they did not know Him. He would not have forgiven
them if He had not loved them. If we turn to Him, want

to love Him and ask for forgiveness, we may be sure that our sorrow for the wrongs we may have done will bring us closer to Him and, with that closeness, bring us peace of mind.

Second Word

"This day thou shalt be with me in Paradise"

It was peace of mind, forgiveness and salvation which he whom we call the 'good thief' knew at the moment of his death. "Lord, remember me when thou comest into thy Kingdom", he prayed, and his prayer was answered at once: "This day thou shalt be with me in Paradise". The other criminal had not wanted to repent. He cursed God, and taunted His Son. "Save thyself, he said, and us too, if thou art the Christ". We do not know what happened to him, but the other one, the good thief, was guaranteed, there and then, the vision of God, the endless happiness of ecstatic love, and this right at the end of his life. He was not saved from the agony of a cruel death on the cross, indeed like his Master he had to undergo that most cruel of cruel deaths. But when the mind knows peace and reassurance, the pains of the body, agonising and weakening, are not strong enough to trouble the mind or rob it of its inner strength. The pain of the good thief had become the gateway to a new and richer life, the fulness of life. Meanwhile he stood at the threshold, waiting for the old life, with its wounds of sins, to pass as he entered into the Kingdom, which they call Paradise.

So, right at the end, on his deathbed, he turned to his Lord, and was saved. That word of the Lord, "This day thou shalt be with me in Paradise", can be spoken to any one of us, even at the last moment. It is not for us to look back in despair, to see the past as robbing us of our future with God. Yesterday's thief can be tomorrow's saint. Our last breath can always be a sigh for forgiveness – and forgiveness is given and life with God assured.

Third Word

"Woman, this is thy son"

She had been told that a sword would pierce her soul. It was an old man called Simeon who had said it to her when she had presented her Son in the Temple, as the Law prescribed. She had already known what the majority of people in our world know only too well. I mean poverty. Soon she would learn that Herod wanted to kill her Son, and with Joseph she would have to leave her own country, and live away from home in exile. Then when her Son began his work with his people, she was in Nazareth when the villagers tried to throw him over a cliff. She sensed the opposition that grew up against him, that opposition which turned into hatred, even though many followed him and received him with enthusiasm. The officials among the religious leaders wanted to silence him. He was in danger. She feared for him.

Then his 'hour' came, that moment when he was mocked and insulted, cruelly tortured, and finally executed in a manner that was both brutal and humiliating. She stood by him; his 'hour' was hers too; and as he suffered in mind and body, she would make his agony her own. A mother makes her own the pain of a son or daughter, and the mother's pain is more keenly felt as if in sharing it she were able to take it away from the one she loves.

So she stood at the foot of the Cross with the beloved disciple John and two or three of her friends. She had watched it all. And she saw the soldier pierce her Son's side after death, and blood and water had flowed. This was symbolising the birth of the Church, the community of those who were to believe, born from the side of a new Adam. Her pain at this birth made her, at that moment, mother of all those who would believe, mother, that is, of the Church. 'Woman, this is thy son', she heard him say as he was dying upon the Cross. He was speaking to her of John, the only apostle present for the others had fled. Mary was to be his mother, and ours too. "Son, this is thy mother". Jesus also had provided for his mother. His dying wish that John should care for her, must surely have been, in part, the healing of her sorrow.

Fourth Word

"My God, my God, why hast Thou forsaken me?"

There are times when we know those consolations or moments of inner peace, which are among God's best gifts, moments when His love seems to touch us deep down at a level within us which none but He can reach. Then there are times when those consolations and that inner peace are no longer there. Our foolishness may have driven them away or our selfishness led us to forfeit them. It is not always so, for He may sometimes wish us to dwell, for a time, in darkness so as to be better able to receive, later on, a greater and stronger light. Faith is tested and purified, so that his love, and no other, may fill the emptiness that is ours.

That emptiness, when God is not in our lives, or so it seems, is a terrible pain. That sense of being abandoned by God is the most crucifying of all pains; it is the end of hope, it is the way to despair, to nothingness. To speak of God's love for us at such moments seems meaningless. It only adds to the pain. If we know that God is with us, there is much that we can endure, for pain and sorrow will pass and joy and peace will return. But if there is no God . . . or if we sense that we have been rejected . . . that is a crushing burden, too much for the human spirit to endure. We can only pray: "My God, my God, why hast Thou forsaken me?" (Ps 22,1). The psalmist's prayer at that moment was the prayer of Christ, and it spoke of the dark experience of abandonment, which was his greatest suffering. How he, who was God, could know such abandonment, such emptiness, we do not know. We can but ponder on the fact in silent prayer. If we are called to share that same experience, and when thoughts and words increase the pain and confusion of our minds, then are we surely one with him. His darkest moment, and ours, are one darkness. Into that darkness comes his light, not ours, but his is given to us to be our peace.

Fifth Word

"I thirst"

He was parched – drained by the pain, the loss of blood and the sweating – he longed for someone to give him something to slake his terrible thirst. But the longing in him was deeper than this. The physical thirst was but the sign of that deeper thirst, the thirst to be able to give God's most precious gift to us, and that is His love, and to receive from us the satisfying of that mysterious need (and this in a manner of speaking) in Him, which is to receive our love in return. Was not his greatest pain, perhaps, the pain of rejection? To be unwanted, despised, to know that others wish to inflict sadness and to hurt, and this at the hands of those who meant so much to him. So he thirsted for them all, as he thirsts for each of you and for me, and at this very moment. That word 'I thirst' is of all the last words which he spoke on the Cross the most personal and the most intimate. It is the revelation of God's great love, at once warm and strong, for us, and for those of us also who have rejected him or despised him.

They gave him vinegar to drink – to dull the pain perhaps – but a bitter drink nonetheless. It will do, so the soldiers thought. A thoughtless gesture, without some sweetness in it, is no true expression of love; it can hurt as much as Judas' kiss, an empty sign because it does not come from the heart.

He longs for me. He thirsts.

Sixth Word

"Consummatum est"

Consummatum est – it is achieved, it is completed.

God's work has been done. "Take away this chalice from before me; only as Thy will is, not as mine is" (Lk 22,42). Your work must be complete, your will be done on earth as it is in heaven. You sent your Son to redeem us, to free us from sin and from death – the wages of sin – to bring peace and, with peace, justice. Your will was to restore in the second Adam what had been lost by the first. Was it not to restore the jungle of human misery to that paradise of happiness which was ours before sin had conquered our innocence and our purity? As we watch your Son die upon the gibbet, do we see there the perfect image and likeness of You, our Father? Is this the perfection of your work, has your purpose been achieved and your intentions brought to completion? The image and likeness of God is sorely distorted and disfigured in the image of His Son, Christ, dying upon the Cross. "Behold the man", Pilate had said, with irony as we would think, and here was man "without beauty, without majesty, no looks to attract our eyes; a thing despised and rejected by man, a man of sorrows and familiar with suffering, a man to make people screen their faces; he was despised . . . how could we take account of him?" (Is 53). So Isaiah, the prophet, said. To this day the image and likeness of God will strike us thus: children distorted by hunger, men and women disfigured by torture and war, civilisation in danger of total destruction, man's greed and cruelty making of humanity something less than human, destroying life, God's precious gift, and thus denying one further finite expression of His limitless beauty. Behold the man . . . God, made in Christ to the image and likeness of man, had become a thing of derision, mocked, scourged and killed. Was this, Lord, the completion of your work, the restoration of man to his original state?

The Father looked upon His Son as he was dying, and rejoiced: "This is My beloved Son in whom I am well pleased". No human, however distorted or disfigured, is despised or rejected by that loving Father, for His scrutiny goes to that which lies deepest within, to the

mind and heart which neither sin nor death can conquer, and where true freedom is to be found, and thus
love, which is freedom's power to want and so to
choose. Man can fetter and conquer what the eye can
behold, but the Spirit remains free and to it is given the
victory. It is that inner freedom which was won upon
the Cross, and the reward for it in Paradise. "Death
where is thy sting?" now that the Spirit has had its
triumph? (1 Cor 15,55).

The Lord has touched our human experience, and
leads it now through the darkness to light, from death
to life . . . to a life of which there is no end and where
the desires of humans are finally and completely fulfilled . . . a happiness given to those who have sought,
only and above all, that His will be done. For such His
work is completed and brought to perfection.

Seventh Word

"Father, into thy hands I commend my spirit"

In Jesus Christ our lives, all that we are and all that we
do, find their true meaning. He, who became one of us,
lived as we do, has made holy all that we are and all that
we do, save, of course, when we sin. He has made our
joys and laughter holy, our daily tasks as well, and so
too our suffering and also our dying. These are now
holy things, sanctified because he has touched them.
Human tragedies, the sorrows and pains of men, of
women, of children, have been given a special dignity;
they contain the promise and the giving of new life.

When pain is most acute, or when there is only
darkness in the mind, or love is wounded, new life is
born within us; it is suffering's gift to one sorely tried
by pain and sorrow. It is like the seed that is in the
ground; it must die before new life can come from it.
The dying of the seed is deep, hidden from view and the
new life is there too before ever it can be seen. We do
not know how that new life comes to be within us –
it may be when our suffering becomes a cry to God for

help; or it may be when our thoughts and actions turn away from what is evil to a life in which God's wishes become our desiring, or perhaps when we resign ourselves into His hands, totally and lovingly. "Into thy hands I commend my spirit". That was Jesus Christ's prayer at the last moment, repeated down the ages by men and women, tortured and killed for their beliefs, the martyrs. That prayer has been said by countless men and women lying sick in hospital, martyrs, too, in their way; by parents mourning a child; by lovers broken through their parting from each other; by people tortured by anxiety and worry; by men and women of great courage and endless patience, each one of them masters of their pain and sorrow because disciples of their suffering Lord. These are the people who have discovered, in the carrying of their cross, the secret of the Resurrection – that new life comes from the dying seed. They have made themselves one with Jesus Christ in his passion and death. They share with him now that new life, the divine life, which was his when he rose from the dead and comes to us at Baptism.

That divine life will grow, if we allow it, and it is often through pain and sorrow that this will happen. We share in his suffering and death, and discover in ours the meaning of the Resurrection. There is no Good Friday experience that does not lead to a greater understanding of and sharing in the joys and triumph of Easter Sunday. Resurrection can become for each of us a daily experience. Every slight pain, every small anxiety, misunderstandings, disappointments and life's contradictions – all of these are experiences of little deaths. Our daily hurts, and every one of them, have within them the joy of Resurrection. If we kiss the crucifix, we shall discover him who suffered like us and for us. That kissing can, sometimes, more easily be done, when words seem empty and meaningless. It is a way of saying "Into thy hands I commend my spirit", and often it is the best way, perhaps the only way. Relief from pain and sorrow may not be immediate; indeed we may be called to walk further carrying our cross, but the yoke will be sweeter and the burden lighter. Of course we cannot, and must not, rejoice in the pain. That would be to do violence to our instincts and to our natures. We are not made for pain; we are made for happiness. But recoiling from the cross, as is natural, we can yet rejoice in the carrying of it, but it must be for his sake, I mean to be like Christ and so with him, he in us and we in him.

There is, to my way of thinking at any rate, no adequate explanation of why there should be suffering in a world made and loved by God. I am baffled by it, and I am sure that you must be as well. The only explanation that makes sense comes, I would suggest, from looking at the image of Christ dying on the Cross, and knowing that the figure of the crucifix was not overcome by death. When the hopes and expectations of his friends seemed to be buried with him in the tomb, new hopes sprang forth from the midst of despair when he rose from the dead. He made all things new, suffering and death as well, your suffering and your death too.

*　*　*　*　*

The power of the Risen Christ

The Resurrection has power to transform our lives. The more we accept its truth, its reality, the greater will be the change in our attitudes towards God and in our view of the world in which we live.

Sin and death did not triumph over Jesus Christ; indeed they could not, for the man Jesus Christ was also God. When one day we shall see God as He truly is, we shall understand the richness and fulness of life itself with all its wonder and all its beauty. We shall realise too that the perfection and the origin of all love is in Him. These things lie beyond us now; they are beyond our understanding. But we can see enough to know that life and love in Jesus Christ could not possibly be extinguished, could not be defeated. With him they would, so to speak, rise again and become then his gift to us.

He wants to give us his love. He wants to give us his life. He will do so if we wish to receive them from him. This is what St Paul meant when he wrote: "Now the life you have is hidden with Christ in God" (Col 3,3). New life has been given to us. We received it first at Baptism. That life made St Paul say on another occasion: "I live now, not I, but Christ lives in me" (Gal 2,20). Bold words but full of significance. We must not think of Christ rising from the dead and then leaving us to cope as best we can, to live as he taught us how. No, he remains with us, present always, unseen by the eyes and beyond the touch of the hand. Through our faith we come to realise more and more his presence within us and around us. Jesus Christ lives.

* * *

The celebration of the great mysteries of our faith, the passion, death and Resurrection of Our Lord, these are not external truths to be celebrated once a year. They are truths which have to affect lives here and now. They have to work their power upon us so that we may be better fitted to be witnesses of Christ today. The world is badly in need of direction and of ultimate vision.

Often we are at risk from those with a single and simple idea. Zealots press ahead relentlessly, reducing everything to a preconceived pattern, suppressing all that they believe to be irrelevant. The vast majority may wake up one day to find our society and its institutions undermined or under control. It is important for ourselves and our society that we retain and develop a sane and wholesome faith, a sense of the eternal and the spiritual, a set of values and attitudes that will respect human dignity and shape a more human society. We need to be armed with faith and vision. We need the courage to withstand all onslaughts. We draw strength not from ourselves and our own resources but from faith and union with Jesus Christ. In our name and for our sake he won a final victory over darkness and death. His Resurrection from the dead is the foundation of our Christian faith. It is God's assurance to us that we will never die and never be ultimately defeated.

*   *   *   *   *

Mother of Christians

There is a tendency today to undervalue devotion to Our Blessed Lady. That is a great mistake.

We should recall that scene on Calvary as Christ was dying. Our Lady was there at the foot of the Cross with St John. Jesus in his dying moments turned to her and said: "Woman, behold your son", and to St John: "Son, behold your mother". It was as Our Lord lay dying on the Cross that the Church was coming into existence. It was the moment when we were being redeemed. As Our Lady was standing there by the Cross, suffering with Our Lord, it was as though she were going through the birth pangs of bringing new life into being. It was the Church that was being born. Mary became at that point the Mother of all Christians.

In the Litany of Our Lady there are three invocations dear to generations of Catholics. We call her "refuge of sinners", a mother's heart always forgiving; "comforter of the afflicted", a mother knows how to be gentle and tender; "help of the sick", a mother knows how to spend herself in the service of one who has need. Surely if a mother's heart is touched by suffering, it is only so

because that is the way God is. God is always touched
by human feelings, by human infirmity. Mary reflects
that.

*   *   *

There are persons with whom from time to time one
comes in contact who have something very special about
them, a transparent goodness so that in their presence
we feel inevitably small and unworthy, persons before
whom one would never say anything base or do anything unworthy. Such was the kind of reaction which St
Peter had on one occasion when he fell down on his
knees before his Master and said: "Depart from me, I
am a sinful man". In the presence of Our Lord that
kind of reaction was inevitable. At the same time, in
people of such goodness there is usually to be found a
graciousness and consideration which, a moment later,
reassures and comforts. So it was with our Blessed Lord.

There is of course only one person who above all
others reflected the nobility, goodness and integrity of
Jesus Christ, and that was his own mother. By the grace
of God, she accomplished and achieved a goodness,
nobility and integrity second only to her divine Son.
The reason for that, of course, was her sinlessness, her
total liberation from any taint of the guilt which has
affected human beings from the time of Adam's sin. She
is, as she told Bernadette at Lourdes, the Immaculate
Conception. For at the moment she began to be, in the
womb of her mother St Anne, she was a new beginning
for our human race, a second Eve, restored to primaeval
innocence because God had willed her to escape the
contagion of sin through the sacrifice of the second
Adam. Her dignity, nobility and integrity were gifts of
God to her for the function she was to perform, to be
the mother of Jesus Christ.

Prayer to Our Lady is part of the Christian instinct. It
must be part of ours. It would be folly to neglect that
prayer which has been said down the ages, the holy

rosary. That prayer has its own attraction and its own value. If we find, as we sometimes do, that we are neglecting the rosary, then a feast of Our Blessed Lady is a strong reminder of our negligence and a prompting of our determination to take it up again. The faithful who pray the rosary always remain close to the Virgin Mary, and those who are close to her can only draw closer to her divine Son.

*   *   *   *   *

Mother of sorrows

I am very struck by two sentences in particular from St Luke about the presentation of the infant Jesus in the Temple at Jerusalem. The first is: "The child's father and mother stood there wondering at the things that were being said about him". The other one is when Simeon had told Our Lady and St Joseph that the infant Jesus was destined to be a sign that is rejected, and said to Our Blessed Lady: "A sword will pierce your own soul too".

I think of Our Lady, sometimes bewildered, sometimes puzzled, often not understanding what was going on and what the deeper meaning of it all was. We are told that she pondered things in her heart. I think too of Our Lady and that sword which will pierce her soul. How strong that phrase is. It sums up all the suffering that she had to undergo, that purification of faith which is the prerequisite of growth in charity.

I think often how people in the Church today, so often find themselves bewildered, puzzled, uncertain, uneasy in their minds. I think too of how so often there is pain in people, often hidden by a brave face. Inside there is deep sorrow and great pain. Of course there is laughter and joy, and a sense of fulfilment in many

different situations in life, but there are also periods of
bewilderment and uncertainty. There are periods when
the sword pierces our soul.

We can have bewilderment in our lives. Sometimes
we can have difficulties about our faith. Sometimes we
can be baffled and puzzled by the way God's providence
is working itself out in our lives, in our families, among
those around us. This kind of confusion can lead to
discouragement, can drag us down and remove, somehow, the sheer joy of living. When that sword pierces
us there can be great pain indeed.

Then my mind moves to that old man Simeon, who
must have learnt much from life's experience, coming
into the Temple prompted by the Holy Spirit, and I
recall his lovely prayer: "Now, Master, you can let your
servant go in peace just as you promised, because my
eyes have seen the salvation which you have prepared
for all the nations to see". At that moment Simeon
understood not only that this child in his arms was the
Messiah, the promised one for whom they had all waited
so long, but he understood too the meaning of his own
life. "Behold, my eyes have seen the salvation which
comes from the Lord". He was praying for something
which we all want deep down: to have eyes to be able
to see, to be able to understand what God wants of us
and for us, to understand what is the great depth and
height of love which He has for each one of us, to be
able to understand the gifts which He wants to give to
each one of us.

How important to have always in the back of our
minds, and to be able to bring to the front in time of
need, this great conviction of God's very special care
and interest in each one of us. That conviction has to be
strong and deep and it comes from a spiritual life led
faithfully, prayerfully and perseveringly. That is the
lesson we learn from Simeon. He was a good and upright
man. At the end of his life he knew peace and understanding.

There will be times when, like Our Lady, we are
puzzled and bewildered. Sometimes there will be

periods when we must walk through life groping, like blind people. When we are experiencing that kind of situation we must stick at it, be faithful, keep going, knowing that God allows this for one reason alone: that we learn to trust Him. It is quite easy to trust when things go well, when we see clearly. But it is quite different when we have to walk in the dark and go on trusting.

When the sword pierces our hearts, we remember that this was Our Lady's experience too, and because it was hers, there should be a part of us that can say "thank you" when we are called upon to undergo the same. She is there – in the background as mothers often are – but there nonetheless.

Baptism and holiness

At Baptism and Confirmation we promise to renounce sin and we make an act of faith. We answer Our Lord's call to "repent and believe the Gospel". The effect of Baptism is to make us in a special manner sons and daughters of God our Father. St John wrote that those who receive Jesus Christ into their lives are empowered to "become the children of God" (Jn 1,12). And St Paul wrote: "God has sent the spirit of His Son into our hearts, crying out in us, 'Abba, Father'. No longer then, are you a slave, you are a son and because you are a son you have the son's right of inheritance" (Gal 4,6–7). We are, then, brothers and sisters of Jesus Christ. When the Father sees you and me, He is reminded of His own Son; there is a family likeness. The divine life within us is hidden from our sight. We see the effect of the life we call grace; we cannot see the life itself.

An early Christian author wrote of the creation of Adam from clay: "Whatever was the form and expression which was given to the clay (by the Creator) Christ was in His thoughts as one day to become man" (Tertullian, De carnis resurrectione, 6). At evening prayer on a Friday the Church sings:

> "In His own image God created man,
> And when from Christ He fashioned Adam's face,
> The likeness of His only Son was formed:
> His Word incarnate, filled with truth and grace".

God created us to His own image and likeness. The model He had in mind was His Son made man, a human like us. The Father wants us to be like His Son. Because of the divine life within us we should, in our attitudes and actions, become increasingly Christ-like.

Now we cannot "belong to Christ unless we have the Spirit of Christ" (Rom 8,9). Recreated, refashioned, remade in the image and likeness of Christ and with his life within us, we are at the same time temples of the Holy Spirit. He is within us; indeed it is only through the Holy Spirit that we can say "Jesus is the Lord". And it is to the Holy Spirit that we attribute the giving of those gifts which characterise the lives of the sons and daughters of the Father (1 Cor 12,4–11).

How do we live out the full implications of being a son or a daughter of the Father, a brother or sister of Jesus Christ, a temple in which the Holy Spirit dwells? It is the attempt to do precisely this that is the striving for holiness. It is our task to become more Christ-like, more sensitive to the promptings of the Holy Spirit. Increasingly we must so resemble Christ that the Father can say of us: "This is My beloved son, this is My beloved daughter; in him, in her, I am well pleased".

That is a sublime ideal; it may well seem unattainable. Certainly at first it appears remote in a life full of daily cares, with work to be done, mortgages to be paid off, worries in the family and a host of other problems. And yet, we would be very wrong to lose sight of the wonderful things written by St Paul about the dignity of a baptised person. Do you suppose that the Romans, Ephesians and the others to whom St Paul wrote, were all that different from us? We have our problems, no doubt, but they had theirs. Furthermore, I doubt whether the Corinthians were a particularly impressive community; rather the contrary. St Paul did not tell the Corinthians that holiness was for other people. And he would certainly not dispense us from the effort to become more Christ-like.

We shall often fail to live up to the ideals put before us by Our Lord in the gospels, and explained to us by St Paul in his letters. That is not too important. Our part is to try, to keep doing our best. There is a whole way of coping with apparent failures in the spiritual life. But I have spoken about this elsewhere.

* * * * *

Friendship with God

Holiness involves friendship with God. God's love for us and ours for Him grows like any relationship with other people.

There comes a moment, which we can never quite locate or catch, when an acquaintance becomes a friend. In a sense, the change from one to the other has been taking place over a period of time, but there comes a point when we know that we can trust the other, exchange confidences, keep each other's secrets. We are friends.

There has to be a moment like that in our relationship with God. He ceases to be just a Sunday acquaintance, and becomes a weekday friend.

* * * * *

Hints on holiness

There will be people, men and women, who will be called by God to devote themselves to service of Him by taking vows of poverty, chastity and obedience in religious life. Some will live what we call the contemplative life; others will be actively involved in the apostolate and in pastoral activities. There will be those, too, who will follow God's call to devote their lives as lay persons, either married or single, content to live on small salaries and in humble circumstances, in order to bring the values of the kingdom of God into our world. Such people are putting into practice the teaching of Our Lord about feeding the hungry, clothing the naked, giving drink to the thirsty (Mt 25,31–46). Others will work, full time, for peace. All of these are much to be admired and supported.

I am speaking now to those who do not fall within these categories. I refer to men and women whose daily energies are absorbed by family problems, their work, possibly bad or problematic living conditions and other such difficulties. They have little time or energy for anything 'extra', either in terms of frequent attendance at weekday Mass or involvement in 'good works' as they are sometimes called. How important it is that these persons should know and appreciate the fact that they too are called to holiness. They too must realise that God wishes to be close to them. We can become holy in any situation or circumstances (except ones that involve sin, of course). It is not where we are or what we do that matters; it is who we are and what we become.

There are a few 'tips' or suggestions which may help you to grow closer to God. There are, I am sure, other ways and means which can help us in our daily lives to become holier people. My 'tips and suggestions' are recommendations only. Other priests or persons skilled in these matters will doubtless have other suggestions to make; in any case, my list is not complete.

These 'tips' read easily enough, but it is not at all easy to make them part of our lives. Again, what matters is that we should try. Do not worry if you fail. Just start again tomorrow. Each day must be a new beginning.

1. Start the day with a morning prayer. Call to mind the different things that you have to do, or which are going to happen. Ask God to give His blessing to it all, to give you help to please Him in all that you do. Tell Him that you want to make all your actions – your work, your recreation, your social life – acts of love. Remember that Jesus lived the ordinary life

of a carpenter of his day. That was pleasing to his Father, so what you do can be pleasing too.

2. If you know that there are going to be moments in the day when things will be difficult (e.g. work will be hard, boring, unrewarding) or times when you will suffer (e.g. from ill health, difficult relationships with others, hard decisions to take) then accept them as crosses which you have to carry this day. Just say: "Thy will be done, dear Lord, not mine. Let all these things bring me closer to Thee". That is how Our Lord prayed.

3. Set aside at least five minutes in the day in addition to morning and night prayers, just to be alone with God. Plan when and where to do this. It may have to be as you go to work; you may be able to find a quiet corner in the home; you may just have to go out and take a short walk on your own. You will recall how Our Lord slipped away from the crowds just to be alone. You must too.

4. During the day things go wrong. For instance: you have been unfairly (or even fairly) criticised; you have been unjustly treated; you have been insulted or just ignored; someone has been unkind to you; you have been snubbed. Those are golden opportunities to grow in holiness. You will probably feel furious and want 'to get your own back'. Try this: bite your lips, as it were, and just say "thanks be to God". You will go on feeling furious, but that prayer, said when you are churned up and upset, is extraordinarily valuable and it does bring a deep peace – eventually. You will have remembered that Our Lord was terribly insulted and hurt, and he just said: "Father forgive them, they do not know what it is they are doing" (Lk 23,34).

5. You will meet all kinds of people today. Some you

will like, others not. You will find it easy to be pleasant to the former, not easy in the case of the latter. What rules of thumb will help us in these situations? I once met a high-powered business man, who told me that he had trained himself always to act towards other people on the assumption that he liked them. If he had a difficult person to deal with, or if he had dealings with one he disliked, he would ask himself: "What would I do if I really liked that person?" He then did it. Remarkable advice, and that way of handling people is entirely compatible with firmness. He was not only acting in a very Christ-like manner, but he ran an extraordinarily efficient and happy business on that basis.

It goes often against the grain to refrain from hurting people, to stifle the urge to gossip unkindly and to ruin reputations. Calumny and detraction are hideous sins; unkindness too offends against the spirit of Christ. Sharp tongues and pens are lethal weapons. Try to see Christ in everyone you meet, and especially in the poor, the sick and the handicapped. Behave towards others as you expect them to behave towards you. That is ancient advice, but very contemporary too.

6. The most powerful means of sanctification are the sacraments. You should make the Sunday Mass the high point of your week. It should be recognised as the most important event in your life. Much of the Mass may be uncongenial to you. I mean it may not be celebrated in a dignified manner; you may dislike the translations of the prayers and the readings; you may find the singing and the music hard to tolerate; you may even find attendance at Mass boring. At one level of our experience, this does, of course, matter; but in fact at another level – the more important one – it should not. The Mass is always the Mass, and the reality of Christ's sacrifice made sacramentally present is always achieved when Mass is celebrated. That is what really matters; that is

what we must grow to understand and appreciate.
Play your part in making the Mass a dignified
celebration. Try to understand what the Second
Vatican Council did in terms of making the Mass
something in which we could share more fully, and
as part of a worshipping community. The important
thing is to go to Mass, take part and pray. Sunday
Mass is essential, but if you wish to grow in holiness,
plan to go on other days too. It is, for many people,
less difficult than they perhaps tend to think.

7. Do not neglect the sacrament of Reconciliation,
'going to confession' as we used to call it. Much
could be said about this, but among these 'hints'
I shall go no further than to remind you that kneel-
ing before the priest confessing humbly our sins,
trying hard to be sorry and receiving God's forgiveness, is a great help to growing in holiness.

8. Holiness is not just a private and personal affair. It
is, of course, a matter of my growing closer to God,
and trying to know, love and serve Him as best I
can. But that is not all. I have to observe the second
commandment of Christ which is to love my neighbour as myself. I have to be involved in serving the
larger community, that is the people who live in my
neighbourhood, and indeed those who live in other
parts of the world. They must all be part of my concern, even though I may not be in a position to do
very much myself.

   Many people simply have not got the time or the
energy to do much more than get through the day,
and care for their families and their own homes. But
I would think that most of us could find close at
hand an old or a sick person whom we can visit once
in a while. We can all become aware of the great
problems of our day: hunger and poverty for the
majority of people in this world, the threat of a
nuclear war, ignorance about God, the neglect of
religion, and unemployment and many others. In

our parishes we should be able to find out more about these things and learn about groups which are involved in playing some small part to help less fortunate people, or to tackle big problems. Great social problems are resolved by ordinary people becoming concerned and doing what they can to find solutions.

A Christian has to be involved. That involvement will be different for different people. We do not all have the same gifts or the same time available for activities outside the home. What matters is to do what we can, however small.

9. Prayer, service of my neighbour, offering my work to God are all part of growing in holiness. Where does 'asceticism' fit in? What are we expected to do by way of works of penance? Is it a wrong view of life to give good things up? Let us be clear: persons and things are good; it is we who misuse them. "God saw that it was good . . ." is the constant refrain in the Bible's description of creation. Man's sinfulness came later. It is good Christian practice to thank God for the sound of beautiful music, for the delight of a glass of wine, for the beauty of a lovely girl. It is a fault to fail to thank God for such things; a fault not to recognise that they are His gifts. And yet it is also part of good Christian practice to say 'no' to ourselves, that is, to deny ourselves good things. We do this lest we fall into the error of thinking that the good things of this life are the only ones that matter; lest, too, we turn persons and things into idols. These false gods will first make us their slaves and then destroy us; or rather, it will happen if we do not exercise self control. What should we do? Clearly this is a matter for individual choice. Friday, the day Our Lord died, traditionally is one upon which we try to do something extra. The new Code of Canon Law has laid special emphasis on our adopting some penitential exercise. These are to be

determined for each country by episcopal confer-
ences. Then there is Lent as the traditional time for
special efforts. It is wise in Lent to take on extra
prayers as well as to give something up.

We usually think of giving up food or drink when
it comes to self-denial. That is still a good way of
approaching asceticism. But there are other possibilities. For instance, we might deprive ourselves of
an hour or so of television once in a while, and do
some spiritual reading instead. We might go to see a
sick or old person instead of doing something we
would enjoy doing. The key is to be able to say 'no'
to ourselves, and this, not just for the sake of saying
'no', but to train ourselves to saying 'yes' to God. It
is this which matters.

It is a false spirituality which regards the good
things of this world as wrong in themselves, or to
think of material things or pleasure as evil. There
have been several heresies about that attitude in the
past. Other people can provide us with excellent
opportunities for self-denial. Being patient, tolerant,
understanding – all that can cost a lot, as anyone
who has lived in community can tell you. It is harder to endure being bored by someone else's conversation than to give up sugar in your tea or coffee!
Other possible ways of saying 'no' to ourselves are
to be found elsewhere among these notes. And in
any case there are enough aggravations in daily life
to provide opportunities for self denial.

10. There is one more 'hint'. It is to remain a little
person. By this I mean: to remain small in my own
estimate of myself, to be unimportant whatever the
position I hold or the talents I have. It is to remember that only one thing matters, and that is what
God thinks about me. To be high in His regard is
the highest ambition any person can have. Smile at
yourself, at your failures, at your spiritual incompetence. Have a sense of humour. It does not matter

if others do not take you seriously; God will.
If you become holy, it is because God has made
you so. You will not know it anyway. Just keep on
trying. That is your part. Success? That is God's
gift. And why not be cheerful? The Lord has risen
indeed, and has much to share with you. You are
precious and important to Him, so why be sad?
There is a French saying which states: "A sad saint
is a poor kind of saint" (Un saint triste est un triste
saint).

*   *   *   *   *

Faith

We walk through life as pilgrims, but we are also like
blind people. We do not see the way ahead clearly. We
depend on others to tell us of what lies ahead, of the
scenery along the road, of the dangers that may threaten
us.

We cannot walk alone. The blind need a guide when
they move in strange places. It must be a guide in whom
they have confidence, one who knows the way and all
about it, and one who will speak the truth. Once the
blind person has found confidence in the guide, then he
will listen and make his own what the guide has said.
Indeed there will be occasions when the blind person
will be moved by what the guide has said and will
love the persons and things about which he has heard.
He believes because he is confident that he has heard
the truth.

We move uneasily in God's world. We do not see Him
and much of what He has told us is far beyond our
understanding. But we are confident that we have been
told truths about God which we could not discover for

ourselves. We accept those truths. Over the years, thinking about them, puzzling over them, we still do not
understand them completely, but at least we appreciate
them more and more. Faith is a question of putting our
trust in the Word of God. In the Scriptures are recorded
truths about God in human words, ideas and stories.
And we have the Holy Spirit present in the Church to
point to the true meaning of the Scriptures. This the
Spirit does through those designated and appointed to
speak with special authority.

I think of those two disciples walking from Jerusalem
to Emmaus (Lk 24,13-35) who listened to the stranger
as he spoke about, and interpreted, the Scriptures. The
eyes of the disciples were 'held fast' and yet they admitted later: "Were not our hearts burning within us when
he spoke to us on the road and when he made the Scriptures plain to us?" They did not realise they had seen
Our Lord, but their enthusiasm had been stirred by his
words. So it will often be with us. We shall often hear
the Word of God proclaimed in Church at Mass and then
expounded by the celebrant. We should listen with real
attention, for it is the Word of God addressed to us. It
can warm our hearts, even if we do not understand
completely. But it is also possible that on occasion the
Word will speak to us in a new way. Familiar phrases or
stories take on a new meaning. The disciples on the way
to Emmaus recognised Our Lord 'when he broke bread'.
It was a moment of special grace. We, too, encounter
the Lord in Word and sacrament, sometimes in a
marvellous manner. It is a meeting that engages us at
every level of our being. Treasure those moments but
do not worry if they are few and far between.

* * *

It would be well to remind ourselves that when we
speak about 'the mysteries of our Faith', we mean
truths about God which we cannot discover for ourselves, and which we can never fully understand. It is

not a question of stumbling into darkness, but rather of walking into the light – a light, however, which is too bright for us to gaze at directly with our weak eyes – just as it is impossible to look directly into the sun. It is too bright and dazzling to see properly. God is like the sun; we cannot see Him as He is. We need someone to tell us about Him, someone who knows and who can be trusted to speak the truth. Our Lord knows, and He has spoken to us. We can say, in our own words, that Our Lord is speaking to us like this: "Listen to me. Trust me. What I have told you is true. You cannot see it for yourself. Stay with me. You have the Holy Spirit. He is in the Church. Stay with me".

The deep conviction we have that Jesus is truly God and truly man is a precious gift from God. So, too, is the conviction that the bread which we receive in Holy Communion, and which we can see and taste as bread, is in fact the Body of Christ. And there are, of course, many other truths which we have made our own, because we have learned to believe in the word of Jesus Christ.

Our lives are greatly enriched by this gift from God, this faith in Jesus Christ. We begin to learn how to cope with all kinds of problems in everyday living by listening to what Our Lord tells us or by seeing what he did or how he reacted to situations. 'Suffering' and 'death' are two clear examples. Such problems, which agonise the minds of so many people, are given new meaning; they are not solved. In Our Lord's suffering and death we find the meaning of ours. Furthermore, we can go through life deriving deeper insight and greater help from those truths of our faith on which we have been nourished from childhood days. For instance, the fact that God became man and dwelt amongst us, died and rose again from the dead – these great facts and many others provide us with food for constant thought. And 'thoughts' will make us want to praise and thank God. Thinking about the truths revealed to us by God in Christ helps us to pray.

Some people find it almost impossible to believe;

even believers experience moments in their lives when doubt seems stronger than belief. Those of us who have to wrestle with such difficulties may be helped by recalling an incident in the life of Our Lord recorded by St John.

Our Lord had been speaking to his followers about 'the bread of life' and, at one point, had said: "My flesh is real food, my blood is real drink". That was hard to understand, and harder still to accept. It is not surprising that we then read: "after this many of his disciples went back to their old ways, and walked no more in his company". That was a blow to Jesus. "Would you, too, go away?" he asked the twelve (Jn 6,69).

We, too, may at times be tempted 'to walk no more in his company'. But if we do that, then we walk alone into the darkness.

When Our Lord said: "Would you, too, go away?" Peter answered: "Lord, to whom should we go? Your words are the words of eternal life; we have learned to believe, and are assured that you are the Christ, the Son of God" (Jn 6,68–69). We can make that prayer our own. It can be a great help and consolation in times of difficulty.

Prayer helps us to believe; faith helps us to pray. These two, prayer and faith, go together and help each other. We pray because we perceive, however faintly. It is prayer, in its many different forms, that enables the dim embers of faith to come to life once again, to enlighten the mind and to warm the heart. An act of faith – "My God, I do believe, help my unbelief" (Mk 9,24) – made when all seems dark and unreal brings with it – perhaps not at once, but gradually – that glimmer of light which is enough. In that flickering light we can walk the next steps of our pilgrimage.

*   *   *

These things weaken our faith: secularism, pluralism and the values of the consumer society.

The prevalence of what is called 'secularism' today is one of those things that makes believing difficult for many. By secularism I mean all those philosophies of life which exclude any explanation of the world and its purpose that has any connection with religion and a transcendent God. Such views can be held by people who are both intelligent and good. We live in a secular society. It is easy to be content for a while with such a restricted view of life even if it fails to provide us with a satisfactory and conclusive vision of human existence.

In a pluralist society we become increasingly aware that society is made up of many races and creeds; there are many other philosophies, many points of view on life. That, too, can weaken the Christian faith. We begin to hesitate, to feel uncomfortable about our religious commitment, to apologise for our beliefs. The Christian voice is but one among many clamouring for the ear of the public.

The values of the consumer society with its idols of wealth and power constitute a real danger to the Christian believer. They have been obstacles to faith right down the ages, and are as seductive today as at any time in the past. They can gradually coarsen the mind and the sensitivity of the believer. We gradually grow accustomed to the easy life and the pursuit of material goals. Ambition and reward become the inspiration of our lives.

Christian education today has to take account of the cultural, social and economic context in which the Christian life has to be led. It has to form a person to be a Christian in a predominantly secularist and pluralist society, with values that are often in contradiction to those which should prevail in the kingdom preached by Christ. That is no easy task, but one that cannot be skirted. The truths of our faith must be taught; the young must be formed to make their Christianity the genuine inspiration and driving force of their lives. In

every Christian there has to be a longing for the desert
and an appreciation of its values and simplicity, even
amid the clamour and pull of the market-place.

*   *   *   *   *

Hope

If ever we ask ourselves what is the meaning and purpose of human life, there is, in the ultimate analysis,
only one accurate answer. It is that man is made for the
vision of God. It is later on, after death, that we shall
become pure contemplatives looking at God who is
truth, goodness, and perfect beauty. Meanwhile we are
waiting for that experience and preparing for it.

When on a pilgrimage, we are encouraged to keep
going because we have the end of the journey to look
forward to. We have already now enjoyed in prospect
something of the joy we shall have in reality at the end
of the journey. We can look forward to good things, to
good times. That is the reason why Christians should
always be joyful, always cheerful. They have hope.
Hope is the confidence that we shall find what we are
looking for, and will reach the point we are aiming at.
That confidence comes from God. It is He who makes
our dreams come true, who satisfies our deepest aspirations, who gives us total fulfilment.

Hope is a Christian virtue and it is as important as
faith and charity. This is not said often enough. People
probably hear many sermons on faith and love, but not
many on hope. Rarely do we see an article on hope, or
see commended to us the importance of being cheerful
and happy, in spite of the trials of life, in spite of the
difficulties we meet. A true Christian would perhaps
say "because of the trials, because of the difficulties".

There has to be in every Christian life a certain joy, a certain peace. I believe many people are depressed more than they should be by the conventions of our mass media. Good news does not sell newspapers, does not make dramatic television pictures. But the unrelieved diet of dramatic crises, of tragedies and conflict, leave many, especially the housebound, the elderly and the nervous, with ample grounds for pessimism and depression.

We must never fail to trust in the love of God, to have confidence that He wants our good. We must be convinced that He wants us, and wants us badly, if I may put it that way.

* * * * *

Charity

"It happened once that a lawyer rose up and tried to put him to the test: 'Master, what must I do to inherit eternal life?' Jesus asked him: 'What is it that is written in the law?. . .' and he answered: 'Thou shalt love the Lord thy God with the love of thy whole heart, and thy whole soul, and thy whole strength, and thy whole mind, and thy neighbour as thyself'. 'Thou hast answered right; do this, and thou shalt find life' " (Lk 10,25–28).

The commandment to love God is clear. We must channel all our energies and selves into that love. It is easy enough to give notional assent to this proposition, but real assent, translated into a programme of action, is quite another thing. We can see our neighbour, but how can we love someone we do not see? The answer is given by St John in his first letter when he writes that it all starts with our realising that God loves us first. When that becomes clear, then we begin to want to love God in return. He has come to us in our nothingness, in our sins, and has loved us to the utmost limit. He suffered and died for us while we were still rebels against Him.

I sometimes think that it is harder for many people to believe that God loves them, than to believe that He exists. The claim that the Almighty cares for me seems almost arrogant. Our behaviour and our constant neglect of Him is calculated to confirm our doubt. But it is good to remember that to forgive is one of the characteristics of true love. One of its joys is to want to help another in his frailty and weakness. To read the story of the wayward youth whom we call the prodigal son is to learn much about the attitude of God towards each one of us. God waits, and always, for our return.

John, the beloved disciple, understood well the strength and warmth of God's love for us and he wrote: "God is love. God's love for us was revealed when God sent into the world His only Son so that we could have life through him" (1 Jn 4,8-9). The understanding of that comes, I suspect, only through a growing appreciation of what Christ Our Lord did for us on the Cross. Love is proved by a man laying down his life for his friend, and what if that man be also God and the friend be still a foe?

I am thinking of the commandment to love God in response to the love which has first been lavished on us. We must understand clearly what is meant. We so often distort the concept of love. We caricature the reality; we deface it; we think of it as a weak, rather insipid, emotion. But the love of which Our Lord speaks is demanding. It is a giving experience, selfless and generous. Love wants to give, as much as it wants to receive, and its model and prototype is the love that is in God.

We learn the power and the urgency of this love of God by looking at the actions and attitudes of His Divine Son, the revelation in human terms of divine realities. He did not spare himself in his service to others. He went so far as to forgive his executioners. Jesus Christ revealed the love which God has for each one of us.

Our own experiences will help too. St John says: "Anyone who fails to love can never have known God, for God is love" (1 Jn 4,8). So all those times, when we have been drawn to others by the goodness and lovableness which we have discovered in them, are precious experiences. They are hints given to us by God of the way He thinks about us, of the way He regards us. Thus, two lovers are especially privileged to be able to explore together the meaning of the love of God.

But love has many levels and human forms. Nonetheless it must characterise all our relationships. I say all, but is this realistic? The lawyer asked: "Who is my neighbour?" and the answer was the story of the Good Samaritan. The man in the parable, wounded and robbed, is the symbol of all men, women and children. My neighbour is every person.

The point is this: we have to try and discover what is good and lovable in all those with whom we come in contact. Each one of us is made to the image and likeness of God. However poor, however sinful, each individual reflects something unique about God. So the more we approach others with sympathy and concern, with the love that God their Father has for them, the more our eyes are opened to see God in them. In this way, the more we love and serve our neighbour, the more we love and serve God. Love of God and love of neighbour grow into a single attitude. Such an approach will undoubtedly make heavy demands on us.

All the time there is ringing in my mind another demand of the Lord, and it is succinct and clear: "Be ye perfect as also your heavenly Father is perfect" (Mt 5,48). It means that if we are to love God and our neighbour, then we must be constantly changing, because we do not and never shall function as we should. We belong to a fallen race; we get it wrong too often. Pride and self-centredness ruin not only the lives of others, but our own too.

So I see this life as a period of training, a time of preparation during which we learn the art of loving God and our neighbour, sometimes succeeding, sometimes failing, but convinced that the ultimate purpose of man's life is the love of God and our neighbour. As we learn that art, many things then begin to look different. Death, for instance, comes to be seen as the way which leads us to the vision of God, when we shall see Him as He is and find our total fulfilment in love's final choice, union with that which is most lovable, union with God.

Perfection for man, then, consists in loving God and his neighbour. Of course there are laws to be obeyed, responsibilities to be fulfilled or undertaken, duties to be done, self-denials to be imposed. These are human tasks from which we easily recoil because they make demands on our time, energies and comfort. Nevertheless, these activities are all part of our religious approach to life. What matters is to have a reason, a motive. We need inspiration. It is love that must inspire.

Religion without the love of God is cold and unreal, it becomes burdensome, and then there is the danger of rejecting it. How often has religion been rejected, jettisoned, because it weighed upon our spirit instead of releasing it?

The love of God and the love of our neighbour, *that* is the heart of it all. It is the secret which all persons must discover for themselves. "Yes, Lord, I do believe; help Thou my unbelief". But I know another prayer, Peter's prayer: "Thou knowest all things, Lord. Thou knowest that I love Thee" (Jn 21,17). This makes good sense when I say "I believe".

*   *   *

When we think of the simplicity of Our Lord's message "To love the Lord thy God with thy whole heart, and thy whole soul, and thy whole strength, and thy whole mind, and thy neighbour as thyself", is it not very odd that love, true love, is so rarely found in this world? Right down the ages we can say that history is the story of our failure to love.

*   *   *   *   *

Prayer

One of the best definitions of prayer is the one in the catechism: "Prayer is the raising of the mind and heart to God". Better perhaps to say: Prayer is trying to raise our minds and hearts to God. If we find that our minds are filled with thoughts that are holy, and if our hearts are moved to want God and to want what He wants, then that is His doing, and not ours. It is His gift. Our part in prayer is to try to raise our minds and hearts to God, to spend time making the effort. 'Trying to pray' is prayer, and it is very good prayer. The will to try is also His gift.

The word 'awareness' is connected with the struggling of the mind to concentrate on God. We are trying to be aware of Him, of His presence, of His closeness. The word 'desiring' or wanting, explains the action of the heart as it struggles to want God. Very often we can desire God, want Him, and our minds can be either quite vacant or full of distractions. That 'desiring' of God can become very strong indeed; 'desiring' without being able to think about God, that too is excellent prayer.

So praying is trying to be aware of God, and being aware of Him, to desire Him, to want Him. As I desire Him more and more then I become increasingly more aware.

*   *   *

Ways to pray

There are different ways of praying. I am speaking at this point about the prayer of an individual, about that prayer which is private and personal. Experienced spiritual directors generally say that the best way for you to pray is the way that you find easiest. I am sure that must be right. Nevertheless we all need help just to get going. There are, happily, several books of recent date which can give you the help you may need. Here are a few suggestions which different people have found to be helpful.

(a) There is a difference between just 'saying' prayers and 'praying' prayers. When you say a prayer try to think either about the words you are reading or reciting, or about the person to whom you are addressing the words. That sounds elementary enough, but it is surprising how difficult it is to do. Remember: your part is to try.

(b) If you take a prayer like the 'Our Father', then spend a few minutes going through it dawdling, as it were, at each phrase. That same way of praying – dawdling through very slowly, and dwelling lovingly on a particular word or phrase – can be used for any of the psalms, for the prayers used at Mass and, of course, for a host of other prayers.

(c) Another excellent way of praying is to use phrases from the gospels, and repeat them slowly again and again. Such prayers as: "Lord, be merciful to me a sinner"; "Lord, I do believe; help Thou my unbelief"; "Lord, Thou knowest all things, Thou knowest that I love Thee"; "Lord, to whom should I go; Thou hast the words of eternal life"; "Thy will be done, not mine"; "Speak Lord, Thy servant listeneth". The gospels are full of examples of this kind of prayer.

(d)   An admirable way of praying the Gospel or, better, of using the Gospel as prayer, is to read a passage slowly. Whenever the name 'Jesus' occurs, or 'he', referring to 'him', then change 'Jesus' or 'he' to 'You' or 'Thou' and change the person to whom Our Lord is speaking to 'me'. In this way your reading of the Gospel becomes a conversation between Our Lord and you. Is not this what it is meant to be? Try it with the account of the blind man being cured, in St Luke's Gospel (Lk 18,35–43).

(e)   The 'prayer of silence' is an important way of praying. You do not use words. You just sit or kneel and try to think about God or some spiritual subject. Every time your mind wanders off to something else, you bring your attention back to go on trying to think about God. It helps sometimes to use a word and repeat it in your mind. Words like 'mercy', 'love', 'forgiveness', 'help', 'holy, holy, holy', 'Come Lord', 'Jesus' and others that you can easily find. Prayer, here, consists in concentrating the mind on the word, and that word, especially chosen by us, connects us at once with something about God. Indeed, it connects us with Him.

(f)   There will be times when we shall just want to stop and enjoy a moment of peace and quiet when, in some wonderful manner, God seems to be very close. There may be such a moment during any one of the ways of praying described above. For example, you may be dawdling through a psalm, saying each verse slowly and thoughtfully, and you find you do not want to go on. You want to stop and just be, and be in the presence of God. That is a moment of grace; it may be very rare indeed, for some it may be quite frequent. I do not know. But when it comes, it is His gift, a moment to savour and one for which to be grateful. It is not, incidentally, a high mystical experience, as far as I know. It happens to beginners and it is an invitation to stick at the business of praying. It is a reward, too, for faithfulness, although we can be very faithful to our prayers with little reward. That last point leads us to consider another form of prayer.

(g)   It is the 'prayer of incompetence'. Most of us know this type of prayer all too well. It occurs when thoughts about God or anything spiritual are quite impossible, and when our desiring is confused and unclear. This kind of thing can happen when we are anxious and worried, full of cares at work or in the home, or perhaps when we are simply 'out of sorts' or unwell. We have no taste for prayer. It would be much easier to omit it altogether. When that is the mood, then we have to make a deliberate decision to pray. Set time aside, survive through all the difficulties, but stay there, just to show God that we want to please Him. There is much merit in that prayer, if little in terms of immediate reward and joy.

(h)   The 'prayer of agony' can be ours when we are suffering. I am thinking in particular about times of sadness and sorrow. It may be the death of someone we love very much, perhaps a terrible depression, or some other affliction that keeps us awake at night and anguished all day. It is on these occasions that we can make our own Our Lord's prayer in the Garden of Gethsemane: "Father, if you are willing, take this cup away from me. Nevertheless, let your will be done, not mine" (Lk 22,42). In other circumstances, when, for instance, we feel that all is lost and ourselves too, we can pray as Our Lord did on Calvary: "My God, My God, why hast Thou forsaken me" (Mt 27,46). So often, when sorely afflicted and sad, it is good just to slip into church and be in agony in the presence of Our Lord in the Blessed Sacrament, and try to say: "Not my will, but Thine be done", or "Dear Lord, I accept this great pain, or at least I am trying to do so. You have asked me to carry this cross. Give me the strength to do so. Simon of Cyrene helped you. Come now, please, and help me".

(i)   Closely connected with the thoughts described above, in the prayer of agony, is that most valuable way

of praying which is to spend time looking at the crucifix. We do not need to say anything; just look, and let it
give up its secrets. It can speak to you of pain, of love,
of patience, of peace in the midst of turmoil. It can tell
of the horror of sin, of man's cruelty to man. It will
remind you of those millions of people who have not
enough to eat each day, of men and women caught up
in wars and revolutions. It will bring to your mind all
those who have died or are dying, of countless numbers
of persons sick in hospitals, of the bereaved; the list of
persons suffering here and now is endless. All of them
are in some manner on that Cross with Christ. That God
made man should die on the Cross is hard to accept;
that a loving God should permit suffering is a real problem. There is only one way to understand these things;
look at the figure of Christ on the crucifix. Behind it,
with the eyes of faith, you can see, can you not, the
outline of the face of the Risen Christ. That glimpse of
the Risen Christ makes sense of that much loved Christian symbol: the crucifix. It is perhaps the greatest aid
to prayer that we possess.

j) In a general way these notes about prayer follow, as I
sincerely hope, the teaching of the spiritual masters of
this subject. I would like to add a further point. We are
always, in prayer, trying to reach a person. We may
address the Father or the Son or the Holy Spirit, as we
wish. If we use words or images these are but means, not
ends. We go through the words to the Person to whom
the words refer or to whom the words are addressed.
If we are praying with our imagination or thoughts
rather than with words, then we go through the image
or through the idea to the Person. It is to a Person that
we try to raise our minds and our hearts. Let us take a
simple example: we say "Our Father, who art in heaven. . .". We can have all kinds of thoughts about our
Father, but we need to go beyond the thoughts to the
Person of the Father. We speak to Him, present to us,
but we are hopelessly let down by our senses. We do
not see, hear, smell or touch Him. We are just aware that

He is near us, and we want Him to be close to us and us to Him. The more we go on in the dark, as if sitting with Him in a darkened room, the more we shall become aware of His presence.

(k) There is an obvious objection. We do not see God or hear Him. Are we not just speaking into nothingness, deceiving ourselves that He is present when He is not? We are like blind and deaf people; we do not see Him and we do not hear His voice. But we just know that He is present and that suffices. I imagine that it might be like this: I am sitting in a dark room with someone I love very much. I do not see that person, for there is no light; I do not hear her voice, for we are not speaking. I just know that she is present. She is happy to be in my company and I am happy to be in hers. We are enjoying each other. That experience can suggest how it can sometimes be in prayer.

So we do not see God, hear His voice or hold His hand. We just know that He is there. He does not speak. Sometimes we speak to Him, using on some occasions a formula, a psalm or a short phrase from the Gospel, on others just speaking in our own words, pouring out our hearts. Sometimes we remain quite silent and still, knowing that He is there and wants our presence. Then, with no words said by Him and no sight of Him given to us, we seem to become more and more aware of His presence. That awareness may last but a moment, on other occasions it may last longer. I suspect that there are people, men and women, and busy people too, who know this experience. Certainly there are those who can speak with more authority about the joy and peace of the higher experiences of awareness and love of God. They will be our masters.

I am quite sure that there will always be moments of inner peace and joy as a result of spending time in prayer for those of us who do not regard ourselves as greatly advanced in the spiritual life. Nevertheless, the experience of many of us is that prayer can be very hard work indeed. Quite often prayer is unrewarding and there is not much joy in the doing of it. It is at moments like these that we can be tempted to give it up. That would be the fatal mistake. We have to keep going. One reason is this: we are learning that an important part of prayer is to please God. We want to please, so that is why we pray. Carrying on when we seem to be getting nowhere is a proof of our faithfulness to God, and it shows that we are selfless and generous in our service of Him. We are prepared to do the right thing for His sake, and not for ours.

From time to time our motives must be purified and so must our hearts. We shall be asked, perhaps, to experience only darkness in our prayer life. We find ourselves without any support. Nothing is of any avail. Spiritual books, fine thoughts, great sermons – they leave us cold and unresponsive. That can all be very disappointing when we can honestly say that we have done our best to be faithful to prayer. There is a reason for this too. Our faith is being purified. This means that we are being led to trust less and less in ourselves, in our own ideas about God, and more in God Himself, and in God alone. We have to go through these periods of darkness in order to be able to receive His light. And when faith is purified (and it can be a painful process) charity increases. We love more.

*   *   *

Planning to pray

How do we set about praying? Perhaps you will regard that as an unnecessary question, or at least one that does not apply to you. Surely, you will think, much of what has been said in these notes applies only to those who are in religious life or have enough leisure to be able to devote so many hours each day to religious exercises.

It would be very wrong to belittle the difficulties of the average family, by which I mean the family in which husband and wife go out to work and the children come back from school hungry. Can the busy housewife find time to pray? Can the man on shift work who returns home tired out and jaded? Let us be clear about this; the basic principles of prayer are the same for the contemplative nun as they are for the busy housewife. The former has more time and a structured life which makes the opportunities for prayer easier. But it would be a grave mistake to hold that prayer is only for certain people and not for others. We all need to pray. Prayer is to the life of the spirit what breathing is to the life of the body.

Of course, there is the prayer in which we share at Sunday Mass, and the importance of that is not to be minimised. But we all need something more. Like Our Lord we need to escape from other people and general business to be alone with God. That 'escape' has to be planned; it has to be organised. We need to find a suitable time and a convenient place. That is not always easy. But perhaps if it were the accepted fact in the family that all its members needed to find time and space just to be alone and quiet, then the organising of it would be much easier. That approach might be too idealistic. In that case each individual should be able to find perhaps no more than five minutes to be alone with God. It may have to be done outside the home, on the bus, walking to the shops, during a tea break. What matters is the planning of just five minutes in twenty-four hours, given over to being alone with God. Is that really impossible? Some will be able to find more time for this personal and private prayer. A quarter of an hour a day, or even half an hour, would be ideal.

Old people and those who have retired from work, or those whose children have now grown up should, as they grow older, learn once again the elementary rules of prayer, or practise with greater ease what in busier times was not possible.

Those five minutes or more should be in addition to

the daily morning and night prayers. These should never be omitted; we need to start the day with prayers and end it in the same way. And the suggestions already made on how to pray apply as well, of course, to morning and night prayers. It is better to say one or two prayers slowly and thoughtfully rather than several too quickly and with insufficient concentration. From time to time during the day it is good to send quick messages to God – short prayers to raise our thoughts for a brief moment to God. That too needs to be organised. For instance, you can decide to say a quick prayer every time you go through a certain door in the house, or when you go upstairs, or as you leave the house. It is an astonishing, but true, fact that you have only to decide to do something of this kind to forget within a matter of minutes. But that is no reason for not trying, and for not starting again.

We need to plan in order to pray. Leave it to your mood and you will discover how quickly you get out of the habit, or simply never pray at all. Few of us pray naturally. You have to get used to it and then you cannot give it up. Prayer is an acquired taste – at least, for most of us it is.

*   *   *

Effects of prayer

We pray in order to be closer to God. I would prefer to put this differently and say: I want to put aside each day just a few minutes, so that God may draw closer to me. This already shows one important result of our praying. God is in touch with us, as friends can be in touch, making known to us what He wants of us. We begin to sense, almost by instinct, what is pleasing to Him and what is not.

Furthermore, we begin to understand things about

Him which we did not before. For instance, we may suddenly realise how much He wants us just from reading about Our Lord's attitude to people in the Gospel. What was once just a story which might have been told by an acquaintance, becomes a personal message from one who is fast becoming a firm friend.

Again, the result of prayer will be to keep God and His will for us at the top of our priorities. We shall, too, be more sensitive to the needs of other people and be moved to do something to help. If we keep our eyes on God, we cannot fail to see the needs of our neighbour.

Wisdom and understanding are the fruits of prayer. We become clearer about the end to which we are travelling on life's pilgrimage, and more certain of the means to be adopted to get there. And however rough the going becomes, we have the courage to go on, remaining deep down at peace.

*   *   *

Prayer of petition

What about the answers to our prayers of petition? How often have we prayed hard for something, and our prayer has been ignored, or so it would seem. And how irritating this is when we have been told quite clearly: "Ask, and it will be given to you; search, and you will find; knock, and the door will be opened to you"(Mt 7,7).

Is there such a thing as unanswered prayer? I am not able to give an answer that convinces me completely. The Gospel passage about asking is clear enough. I am helped by two things. The first is this: just outside Fribourg in Switzerland there is an ancient shrine to Our Lady. It is a holy place and one where it is easy to pray. The walls are covered with expressions of gratitude for answers to prayers said in that chapel. One plaque caught my eye especially. It said: "Thank you for not answering my prayer". What had that person in mind? Did he or she realise how the answer required might have turned out to be harmful? Did that person realise that God's way of handling the problem was wiser and better? I do not know, but that prayer chipped into a stone hanging on that chapel wall was, for me at any rate, an important lesson. God's ways are not mine. He knows best. I do not know His plans, I often do not understand them. I must learn to trust.

How often have we prayed for, say, the recovery of a sick child, and the prayer seems to have been unheard. The child has died. There is no easy explanation of that. But we do have to trust, and that will mean in a situation of this kind, walking on in the darkness and in pain. God had a plan for that child and we do not know and we cannot understand it.

The second aid to understanding apparent failure to answer my prayer of petition is to reflect on what God really wants for all of us. He has one over-riding wish for us, and that is union with Him. Everything else is subordinated to that. So I would think that any request made, which will lead to union with God, either here and now or later on when I shall see Him face to face, will be most certainly answered. Perhaps much that we ask for will not be helpful. But even the asking draws me closer to Him.

I remain a bit uneasy. I do think that what I have written above in these notes is true. Why, then, am I uneasy? It is because the prayer of petition must come from a heart that trusts, from the kind of faith that is strong enough to move mountains. I had to add this reflection. My explanation of why prayers remain unanswered is in many situations true and valid; at other times, though, there may be too little faith.

* * *

Ten golden rules

1. Plan to pray; do not leave it to chance. Select a time and a place (a room at home, on the bus, taking a walk).

2. Decide on how long you will spend in trying to pray (five minutes, ten, fifteen, thirty or more).

3. Decide what you are going to do when you pray – e.g. which prayer to select to say slowly and lovingly; or which passage from the Bible to read prayerfully. Sometimes use your own words; sometimes just be still and silent. Follow your inclination.

4. Always start by asking the Holy Spirit for help in your prayers. Pray: "Come Holy Spirit, teach me to pray; help me to do it".

5. Remember you are trying to get in touch with a Person, and that Person is God – Father or Son or Holy Spirit. He is wanting to get in touch with you.

6. Don't be a slave to one way of praying. Choose the one that you find easiest, and try some other method when the one you are using becomes a burden or doesn't help.

7. Don't look for results.

8. If you have distractions, then turn your distractions into your prayer. (If a car passes the window in the wrong gear, then say something to God about the driver – I mean a kind prayer for the welfare of the driver, not necessarily for his driving or gear box!)

9. If you always feel dry and uninterested at prayer, then read a spiritual book or pamphlet. An article in a Catholic paper may be a help. Spiritual reading is important.

10. Trying to pray *is* praying. Never give up trying.

*   *   *

Perseverance in prayer

Sometimes there will be periods when we are in the desert, when there is no refreshment, moments when we have to hang on through the darkness with our faith. But if we persevere, then from time to time God gives us a sense of His presence. That sense of His presence may be rare. In some people it may be more frequent than in others, but we must always seek the God who gives consolations and not ask or seek the consolations of God.

Stairs have a lesson to teach. I think of a small child learning to walk, and the father is at the top of the stairs. The child is not yet old enough, indeed is too weak to climb those stairs on his own. Every time he puts his foot on the first step he falls over backwards. He tries it several times with unfortunate and unsuccessful results. The father is standing at the top of the stairs watching. Now, the child has a number of options. He can sit down at the bottom of the stairs and howl with frustration and fury (when did I last howl with frustration and fury?) because he can't do it. Or he can take another option and say this is no good and push off into another room. So it is either getting angry or giving up. But the father wants to see the child go on trying to get up the stairs. It's obvious what must happen. Since the child is too weak, but showing willing, then the father goes down the stairs, picks up the child and carries him to the top.

That is the way it is. Our part is to go on trying, putting our foot on that first step, painfully, doggedly. Then from time to time the Father will come down, pick us up and carry us to the top. In God's way of doing things, if He ever does carry us to the top, He then always puts us back again at the bottom of the stairs to start all over again. It is only right at the end of life that He takes us to the top and keeps us there.

So there are times when, if we go on trying, God will take us to the top of the stairs and we sense His presence and know that we are close to Him. It does not last. We are back at the bottom of the stairs again. I don't know how often it is that He will come down and take any of us to the top. We must not be disappointed if it is only once in thirty years. I would be slightly suspicious if it were every other day! I believe that truly valiant souls very often spend most of the time at the bottom of the stairs, just trying to put a foot on that first step. It is pleasing to God to see that constant trying, that constant effort.

Sometimes He gives us some encouragement. For instance, He can smile at the top of the stairs, or make a friendly gesture. There are all sorts of ways in which He can make Himself present, even though we have not got that closeness which we would like and want.

*   *   *

Alone with God

There is one aspect of Christ's life which needs to be constantly underlined and emphasised. From time to time he would withdraw from the crowds and his ministry to be alone with his Father. In that way he showed us the importance of *our* being alone with the Father.

Silence and solitude were part of the life of Our Blessed Lord. In his public ministry, intensely busy, he went off to look for solitude, silence and stillness.

We should do the same from time to time, just to think about the love God has for us. Go back to that constantly.

*   *   *

Mount Tabor and Calvary

We hear the words of Micah: "Come, let us go up to the mountain of Yahweh, to the Temple of the God of Jacob, so that He may teach us His ways and we may walk in His paths" (Mic 4,2).

We go up to the mountain of God, our hearts and minds raised to be with Him in prayer, so that when we come down from the mountain we can walk and labour in the valley in His service.

There are two mountains, Tabor and Calvary. Mount Tabor is the scene of the great Transfiguration when Peter, James and John found it "good to be with the Lord". But we are only able to climb Mount Tabor when we have exercised ourselves climbing that hill which is called Calvary.

When Our Lord calls us to serve him, he does not promise an easy way. He calls us to follow him with courage, with tenacity, in the face of all difficulties. The call is unmistakable.

Do not be afraid of Calvary. Over that hill you come to another one, a different hill, and a friendly one. There you will find a tent where you will remain forever.

* * * * *

Some Sacraments

In the gospels those who were sick came to Our Lord to be cured; the blind man, the one who was deaf and dumb, one suffering from paralysis, another suffering from possession by the devil. Every kind of illness was brought to Our Lord for healing. He stretched out his hand to touch them and they were healed.

Every touch of the Lord on those sick people cured them of their illness, and gave them renewed life. He healed, enlivened and the life he gave was the life of God.

That is one way of understanding the sacraments; they are ways in which we receive his touch and live.

Each sacrament is a saving encounter of the individual with the living Christ. Each brings a special help, an infusion of new vigour in particular circumstances, at particular times, to meet particular needs. The symbolism of each sacrament reveals its particular power. They are celebrated within the community of the Church, but at the heart of each sacrament the believer is alone with his redeeming Christ. The pastoral visit of Pope John Paul to England and Wales revealed to many people unsuspected depths and richness in the sacraments. That precious experience must not be allowed to fade.

* * *

The Mass

We pray alone, we pray also as a worshipping community, we pray at Mass, we pray whenever we receive the sacraments.

The Church and the Eucharist are so closely connected that you could almost say one explains the other.

When I think of Jesus Christ I think, with St Paul, of the body of Christ of which we are the members and he is the head; when I think of the body of Christ I think both of the Church and the Eucharist. I feel deeply this relationship, for after all the Church is communion and the Eucharist too is communion. The Eucharist is the high point of the life of communion.

We must not waver in our faith that in each Mass is made present the mystery of Christ's passion, death and Resurrection, and that Christ remains really and truly present for us in the Blessed Sacrament.

One used to say, in my teaching days, that the
difference between faith and theology could be illustrated by what I do before the tabernacle. I genuflect
– why? Because Christ in the Church tells me he is truly
present in the Eucharist. How he is present? That is
theology, and the theologians can never fully explain
it.

Belief in the reality of Christ's presence in the Blessed
Sacrament does not come from reading; it does not
come from thinking; it does not come from any man's
skill. It comes from faith, from the humility of mind to
accept and to say 'yes' to what may seem to be un-
believable, namely that the Body and Blood of Christ
is present under the appearances of bread and wine.

* * *

Reverence

There is a sense of the presence of God which should
always fill us with awe, and lead us to an attitude of
respect and dignity in relationship with God our Father.
The Mass is always a sacrifice, the Sacrifice of Calvary
re-presented, made present for us once again so that we
may be, in some manner, involved in it. Here is one of
the deep mysteries of our faith: in his death is our life.

Sacrifice as a concept, as an idea, is always related to
adoration, to worship. Awe and respect should never be
absent from any Mass. Yet there is another aspect
which is no less important. We see it clearly in St Mark's
account of the Last Supper. Although the Last Supper
was a ritualistic meal, the annual celebration of the
Passover, the high point of the Jewish year, nonetheless it was clear that Our Lord was with friends. The
atmosphere was, as it were, more relaxed. This aspect
we call communion, which suggests intimacy, closeness

and love. That aspect of the Mass should always be present too.

* * *

Holy Communion

The Eucharist is the really important moment in our lives when we are together around the altar, praying and praising God, and getting involved in what Christ did on the Cross, what he did in his Resurrection.

Receiving Our Lord in Holy Communion is a moment when we are enabled to recognise who he is and what he is. How important is the precious moment when he is close to us. It is the moment when we must give ourselves to him, as he gives himself to us. It is the moment when he, in his own way will speak to us and encourage us. In his own way too he will give us new strength if, for instance, we have a big problem in the family or in our own personal lives. It is the moment when we can accept from the hands of God a cross to be borne, a difficulty to be faced. It is the moment to say lovingly "Yes, I will, with Your help".

The moment of receiving Our Lord is a very personal one. It should not be rushed or invaded by distraction. There should be a short time when we are alone with Our Lord. It is only when we can be alone with him, deep down within ourselves, that we can then begin to form a true Christian community, which is, of course, what a parish should be.

Moments of silence and stillness after Communion are important – those moments we spend together before the final prayer and blessing, and those other moments when we stay behind in church – alone with him.

* * *

The Eucharist and faith

The Church encourages us to think about the various ways that Our Lord comes to us. We think first of that historical event when Jesus Christ, the Second Person of the Blessed Trinity, became man and dwelt among us. Our thoughts turn once more to what he did for us by dying on the Cross and rising again from the dead, so that we may have new life within us. We call this, his saving work, the redemption.

Then there are the other ways in which Christ comes to us: through his word in Scripture; through his grace in the sacraments; as a friend in our personal lives – a friend who is seeking intimacy and closeness with each of us; and in so many ways through each other. However, at this time, I want to think particularly about his coming to us in the Eucharist.

Now the Eucharist, the Blessed Sacrament, the Body and Blood of Jesus Christ, is a special gift from God to the Christian community. The Eucharist, as Sacrifice – which is the Mass – is the way that we become involved in a special manner in the death and Resurrection of Our Lord, that is, in the redemption. The Mass makes it possible for us to unite ourselves with Jesus Christ's Sacrifice of himself to his Father. During it we, too, dedicate ourselves and all that we do, to God. The Eucharist as sacrament – as Holy Communion – enables us to be united more closely to Our Lord, and in him with one another. The life of Christ which we first received at Baptism, is sustained and grows through being nourished by the Body and Blood of Our Lord.

When we speak of the Eucharist we think, then, of the Mass at which we receive Holy Communion and also of the continuing presence of Our Lord in our tabernacles. The Eucharist is at the very centre of the whole Church. It should be at the centre of the life of each parish, and of every person in it. It is the Church's most precious treasure. It must be ours. The Mass meant so much to our English Martyrs. They risked so much just to be present. I feel just a little ashamed when I think how devoted the English Martyrs were to the Mass. But these great people inspire us to find out more about the Mass and to love it as they did.

I have even heard people say that they are 'bored' at Mass. That is distressing. I know that some people regret the changes that have been made in the way that Mass is celebrated. That, too, is distressing. Do let us be clear. The Mass of today – the Sacrifice of Christ renewed – is the same as the Mass of yesterday. The changes introduced by the Church are meant to help us to take a more active part in what is taking place. That active part must, of course, be the expression of a truly religious spirit. The Mass requires careful preparation and a reverent and dignified celebration. It is the high point of lives that are prayerful. Its secret is revealed gradually to those who persevere.

Before we can begin to appreciate all the riches contained in the Eucharist, we have to start by renewing our act of faith in what it is. Why, for instance, do we genuflect to the tabernacle on entering the church? Why is it important to show reverence to the Blessed Sacrament? When the priest takes the host into his hands at Mass, and says: "This is my Body which will be given up for you", the bread is changed into the Body of Christ. When he takes the chalice filled with wine and says:

> "Take this, all of you, and drink from it:
> this is the cup of my blood,
> the blood of the new and everlasting covenant.
> It will be shed for you and for all men
> so that sins may be forgiven.
> Do this in memory of me"

the wine is changed into the Blood of Christ. Christ, Our Lord, is now truly present in a special, indeed in a unique manner, amongst us. My eyes see bread and wine; my hands touch bread; and, as I eat and drink, I taste bread and wine; but, in fact, they are the Body and Blood of Jesus Christ. What precisely has happened, we do not know. How exactly this has been accomplished, we cannot tell. Only one thing is certain: what was once bread, is now the Body of Christ; what was wine, is now his Blood. He told us that this is so, and that suffices. The priest at Mass has done what Our Lord first did himself at the Last Supper. We do it in memory of him.

If you are troubled, sometimes, by doubts, and your mind cannot rise above the testimony of your senses, that is, if your faith in the real presence of Christ in the Eucharist has grown weak, then try this. Kneel before the Blessed Sacrament, and say: "My Lord and my God. I do believe; help Thou my unbelief". It works. And, then, reflect that in this, as in so many things concerned with God, understanding comes with practice. We get involved first, and then we begin to see the point.

Boredom is like being in a cloud. We cannot see clearly, nor can we feel the warmth of the sun, but if we go on, sooner or later there will be a chink in the cloud and a little light and warmth will come upon us. That is a moment of joy. But meanwhile ours must be the ideal of the early Christians who – so we are told – "persevered with one accord, day by day, in the Temple worship and, as they broke the bread in this house or that, took their share of food with gladness and simplicity of heart, praising God and winning favour with all the people" (Acts 2:46–47).

*   *   *

Do this in memory of me

When we have made our act of faith in the presence of Our Lord in the bread and wine now changed into his

Body and Blood, we are able to explore a new world, as it were. We begin to discover why it was that Our Lord told us to "do this in memory of him".

Our Lord first changed bread and wine into his Body and Blood at the Last Supper. He was celebrating the Passover meal with his apostles. Year by year, this was the special moment of remembrance and thanksgiving for the Jewish people. They recalled their flight from the slavery of Egypt and thanked God for his deliverance and his protective love on their journey to the promised land. For them, the Passover meal was not simply the recalling of a past event. It was their chance to enter fully into their family history and to make it their own. When they remembered God's goodness to their forefathers in Egypt, they praised and thanked Him for their own freedom, too. Now, during that Last Supper, Our Lord gave thanks and praise to his Father and then changed the bread and wine into his Body and Blood. By so doing, he gave that meal a new meaning. What was it? Our Lord was thinking of another 'saving event' and that was his own death, Resurrection and ascension. He was arranging for its special remembrance in a new kind of Passover meal. From now on, each time one of his priests celebrates Mass, the great event of his redeeming act is made present to us and for us again. We obey his command: "Do this in memory of me". Let us look at this more closely.

Christ wanted us to be involved in what he did for us when he died on the Cross on Calvary. He was full of love for his Father and for us. That love for his Father made him want to accept even death on the Cross to show his obedience. Obedience to another is often a sign of love. I want to do what the one I love wants. We should ponder this, for it is difficult to understand why exactly the Father allowed his Son to suffer so much, and in this way to show his obedience. It tells us something about how dreadful sin is, and something about how much God loves us. We are sinners. Sin separates us from God. The wages of sin is death. Instead of sin, (separation from Him and death) God, in His mercy and love, wants to give us forgiveness, union with Him and life. Christ went through the terrible experience of a cruel death in order to overcome sin and death, so that we, too, might overcome sin and death and enjoy the happy experience of his forgiveness and Resurrection. His obedience, even unto death, brought us freedom and life, the freedom and life of the sons and daughters of God. His death on the Cross for us we call his 'sacrifice'. Each time the Mass is celebrated, Christ's Sacrifice on Calvary is presented again. In a wonderful way, what he did once and for all on Calvary (and Christ cannot die again) is made present for us here and now. It is his sacrifice which we offer to God each time Mass is celebrated. God's forgiveness, new life, close union with Him, are gifts given, and given in full measure, to those who, like Christ, give themselves wholly and generously to God.

How much we should treasure the Mass. We shall never fully understand it, nor cease to discover new things in it. But if we think often about the Last Supper and about Christ's Sacrifice on the Cross, we shall certainly come to appreciate more and more what happens when we "do this in memory of him".

* * *

One heart and one mind

To take an active part in the Mass, I have to worship God by praying. I must also listen carefully to the readings and to the Gospel. These are God's message to me. At times, something I hear will evoke a response in me. It will come like a light to help me to understand something which had not occurred to me before, or it will warm my heart giving me fresh courage, or more love for God. When the prayers are being said, I should try to make them my own as sincerely as I can. During Mass I also offer myself to God. The offertory procession is a good time to do this. Although we cannot all go up to the Altar carrying gifts, representatives do it on our behalf. But this is the moment when I can pray: "Lord, here I am. I give you my work, my joys, my sorrows, my family. . . ". All those personal and private matters will then become Our Lord's as well as ours, when that bread and wine become his Body and Blood. There is much, then, that we can do to make the Mass our own personal prayer, and from each Mass I should go home a changed person, a better Christian.

However, as you well know, we are not simply individuals, only concerned for ourselves. By nature we are related to one another by ties of blood, of friendship, of social relationships. As human beings, we have much in common and we need each other. As the people of God, however, there is a further important and profound reason for regarding ourselves as belonging to a community. It is that we all have the same life in us, uniting us, binding us into one – just as the sap gives life to the whole tree, to each individual branch, and as the different parts of a body share in the life of the whole. Our Lord said: "I am the vine, you are its branches" (Jn 15,5). St Paul described this close relationship in terms of a body: "Just as a human body, though it is made up of many parts, is a single unit because all these parts, though many, make one body, so it is with Christ . . . . Now you, together, are Christ's body; but each of you is a different part" (1 Cor 12, 12–27).

The invisible unity of the believing community – Christ's body, the Church – becomes visibly present when we gather around the altar at Mass, each of us receiving the same food and drink, Christ himself. This Holy Communion unites us with Christ and with each other. This is why the Eucharist is the perfect sign of unity, of many becoming one. Even the elements used indicate this: bread is made from many ears of wheat; wine from many grapes.

It will not, I trust, be out of place to say how sad it is

that in recent years there have been great differences of opinion about the way Mass should be celebrated. There has been disunity where unity should be most evident. Many feel deeply on this subject and this is a sign that the Mass is very important to them. That is good. Perhaps the changes were introduced too quickly, even, possibly, a bit insensitively, certainly without adequate explanation and preparation. I have much sympathy with those who have found the changes difficult. But I have no doubt in my mind that the changes made were right, and I welcome them. One of the aims of the Council Fathers was to secure the active and whole-hearted involvement of the entire congregation at Mass. Most of us have still a long way to go to understand what the Council was trying to achieve.

I must add a further point: I am most anxious that the Mass should be celebrated always with dignity, reverence and in a prayerful manner. At Mass, our minds and hearts should be raised to that which lies beyond and above us. I mean by this that we must be led to perceive, albeit in a glass darkly, the mystery which God is. The longing in all of us to know that which is most lovable and most beautiful must, so I believe, be awakened and satisfied when we attend Mass. We must sense that we have been in the presence of the holy.

Finally, I would say to all: the changes in the Liturgy will only make sense to us if these changes are accompanied by that profound change in ourselves, that renewal of fervour and devotion, to which every Christian in every age is called. There is, too, a task to be done in every parish: it is the building of a community with one heart and one mind, founded upon the love of God and of man, with Christ Our Lord as its cornerstone.

*   *   *

Confirmation: some notes for the young

There are good trees and bad trees. There are trees which produce good fruit and trees which produce bad fruit; that we all know. But the really important things about them are the bits you do not see; they are underground, the roots. If the roots are rotten the tree is no good; either its fruit will be sour, or it will produce no fruit at all.

The bits you do not see are really important. You have to look after the roots; they need water and sometimes in very wet soil they need a bit of draining. If there is something wrong with the tree, you begin by checking on the roots.

The point should be clear. If we are to be like the good tree and produce fruits of joy, peace, love and kindness, then the roots have to be right. We have to be the right kind of people, and that is not always easy; we need help. The ideal person, the model we must follow, is Our Lord Jesus Christ. He is the model; he is the teacher; he gives the example. Yet in order to understand what he was trying to say, and in order to do what he is telling us to do here and now, we need help.

You will find that the older you get the more help you need because there are all kinds of things that can make a tree go rotten. We meet all kinds of things that make us go bad. We need help in particular when we cease to be young people and begin to grow up. The grown-up world is not an easy world, and if you want to be faithful to Christ, if you want to live seriously as a Christian, you are in for a struggle. It will often seem easier to turn round and run away.

So we realise that we need help to follow Christ and to be faithful. At Baptism we become members of God's family; sons and daughters of the Father; brothers and sisters of Christ; temples of the Holy Spirit. At Confirmation we take on new responsibilities in the Body of Christ which is the Church.

You do not see the roots of a tree but you know how important they are. You do not see the Holy Spirit

within you, but he is present, giving you life, Christ's
life.

After the ceremony you might say: "Now I'm con-
firmed, that's that". How foolish that would be. Confirmation is a beginning; you are now an adult Christian.
So you have to be faithful to Our Lord; you have to be
prepared to defend what you know to be true about
God; you have to have courage if you are to witness to
Him, and even if it costs you a lot. That is the purpose
of Confirmation.

*   *   *

In speaking to you about the sacrament of Confirmation, I am first of all going to tell you about a friend of
mine; we shall call him John. It is a true story. John, a
Catholic young man, was selected to play football for
England against France. The team was put up at a hotel
some way outside Paris and on the Sunday morning
John said to the manager: "I'm going to Mass"; to
which the manager replied: "The Church is a long way
off and there is no transport. It is not convenient, you
need not go". But John insisted: "I'm going to Mass".
In the end they picked up a car and he was driven ten
miles or so to Mass.

He told me that story himself, not to show off, but to
try and explain to me how sometimes it was difficult to
go to Mass. But the example he gave, the witness he
gave, did make a big impression on others. He had the
strength to say "I'm going to Mass, whatever you
think". Now, that strength was to be admired. It was
always said that when he came into the dressing room,
if there was bad language or bad stories being told,
everybody stopped. They just felt that in front of him
it was not right. He was not that kind of person. Nonetheless he was in no way a stuffy person; he was a
popular man with a great sense of humour. But he had

also a special strength which enabled him to decide to do the right thing.

Where did that strength come from? It was a gift from God, no doubt. In the sacrament of Confirmation the Holy Spirit comes down and is present in you to give you strength, and the character, to say "Yes, I will go to Mass, even when it is difficult, even when it is inconvenient, even when my mates don't go. I will go in order to please God".

People who have strength respect themselves, and are respected by other people. We badly need in the Church today young people who have that strength. Other people will see in them the kind of person they think Jesus Christ was, because to be a Christian is to try to become more and more like Christ. Just think how different the world would be if we all behaved like Jesus Christ, did the things he did, reacted as he reacted.

When we were baptised we first received the Holy Spirit. When I put oil on your forehead – oil is a sign of strengthening – and say to you: "Be sealed with the gift of the Holy Spirit", you become related to the Holy Spirit in a new way. You are now the special instruments He wants to use for the good of the Church and the sake of the Gospel. But you remain free either to live under His influence, or to say 'no' to Him. So I want you to make up your minds always to say 'yes' to the Holy Spirit, so you always do what you know is the right thing to do.

Remember the reason why there are sacraments. God wants to give us His strength because of His great love for all of us. God loves us more than any parent could love, more than any lover could ever love us, and He wants us to learn about Him and love Him in return. Remember that always. If you do, you will discover that being faithful to your religious upbringing will not be a burden; it will give you real peace of mind, indeed an inner joy and strength that enables you to stand up to all the stresses and strains of life. It will give you freedom of spirit, and that is precious indeed.

The Pilgrim's Tasks

The agenda
The vale of tears
False prophets
Dreams and visions
Building the kingdom of God
A better world
Renew the face of the earth
The Church in the modern world
National values

The issues
Forces of unbelief
War and peace
Christian disunity
Ecumenism: some thoughts
The hungry world

The pilgrims
We are priests
We are prophets
We are kings

Notes on some pilgrims and their tasks
The family
Ideal of motherhood
Work
The Pope and ministry
The priesthood
Priestly jubilees
Vocations
Fostering vocations
Religious life
The sick and the handicapped
The challenge to young people

The Agenda

The vale of tears

The pilgrim's progress today passes through a world of beauty and opportunity. Yet it also winds through valleys of death and cruelty never previously explored. The pilgrim cannot pass by the hungry masses or those who clamour for justice and the recognition of their human dignity. The pilgrim's mind and heart are fixed on far horizons but must never ignore or make light of injustice, pain and deprivation here in the passing world. Each day provides for the pilgrim the tasks that have to be undertaken.

No one need search for a programme of action or a crusade. The world and suffering humanity create the agenda for those who have eyes for human misery, ears for the stories of oppression and degradation and hearts to respond to the distress of our human family.

The pilgrim is confronted with daily evidence of a world of sin and division. Here God is dethroned and empty idols are held in honour. False prophets clamour for attention. Belief and unbelief struggle for ascendency.

Today's world is threatened by new and terrible dangers. Humankind has fashioned weapons which could bring final destruction to our planet. Our race meanwhile multiplies and most face hunger and poverty while the privileged enjoy prosperity unimagined by previous generations.

The pilgrim is not helpless in the presence of such menace and hardship. The divided world can be united and healed. There is an immense work to be done to reconcile divided Christianity, to bring peace and understanding to those who fear and fight each other. There has to be a restoration of family life and the fostering of stable and united communities. These are tasks which involve us all in our different walks of life. They do not distract the pilgrim, nor deflect us from our goal. They are themselves the road we must pursue in our search for God and the fulfilment of His will.

*   *   *   *   *

False prophets

In the West we do not face the same threat to our religious freedom as do our fellow Christians in Eastern Europe. Our danger is not from the person who persecutes in an open and barbarous way, but from false prophets.

False prophets in our time are not necessarily those who deliberately set themselves up to undermine religion and Christian values. But they are the siren voices which help to create an atmosphere, a way of thinking. They say things and preach an inverted gospel which can and does harm society. We are always dimly conscious of what they say; we adapt our attitudes under the pressure they exert. They suggest that there is no other life but the life we know on this earth. They proclaim that there is no God, and indeed that the world and its purpose does not need an explanation which comes from outside.

False prophets are those who will tell us we can find total happiness and contentment in this or that object, in this or that activity. So people can be deceived into thinking that their lives have no other purpose than one to be found exclusively in this life, and that their happiness can only be achieved in the things they can do, and have, in this world.

The prophets, however, prove themselves false because their teaching has already led to disillusion, disappointment and a great deal of unhappiness. The single-minded pursuit of this world, and wrong explanations of it, in the end cheat people.

There is a growing realisation that our Western society has lost its direction and is losing confidence in the guides who have led from one disaster to another. Instead we should be in search of a vision, of noble ideals, of something that is worth living for, and worth devoting our lives to. I sense that people everywhere are longing for a new direction. That should not surprise us, for people are made for God. Without God human life remains an enigma. The deepest hopes and desires of the human heart remain unfulfilled.

*   *   *   *   *

Dreams and visions

"I will pour out my Spirit on all mankind.
Your sons and daughters shall prophesy.
Your old men shall dream dreams,
and your young men see visions" (Joel 2,28)

I am preoccupied not with an old man's dreams, but with his nightmare. A nightmare is a mixture of fear, dread and sadness. I am thinking of someone who late in life has woken up, or half woken up – as is the case in dreams and nightmares – to realise he has dedicated his whole life to the wrong things, or perhaps more accurately has dedicated himself to good things but in the wrong way. He has turned good things into idols. He has become an idolater. He has worshipped false gods.

Power, possessions and pleasure can be false gods. Used rightly they are good things; used wrongly they can, and do, wreak havoc in our lives. For instance, the misuse of power can lead to all kinds of evils, to oppression of the weaker by the stronger, to depriving others of their freedom. It can cause fear in others, and fear leads to hatred and hatred leads to violence. If we think of the misuse of possessions, people can be so eager to have things for themselves that they fail to notice those who have not got enough. There is nothing more depressing than to wake up and find that, after all, the nightmare is true.

Let us listen again to the voice of God: "I will pour out my Spirit on all mankind. Your sons and daughters shall prophesy". What dreams do people have today? People are groping towards a vision of what our society could be like. We dream of a perfect society in which peace reigns, of a society in which the dignity of every person is respected, where freedom prevails and is responsibly used, where respect and true love characterise all our relationships and where life itself is honoured and treasured.

Can dreams become visions? Can visions become programmes for action? It is a sad day when a person ceases to be an idealist. It is sad too for society when it loses its clear vision. There always have been men and women who have dedicated themselves to great causes. Today many campaign vigorously for peace. Others work tirelessly for the protection of life from the time of conception to the end of life. Some are committed to providing housing for the homeless, to feeding the hungry, to protecting the environment. They are often prophets sent to the modern world. They are sometimes uncomfortable people; quite often they are voices crying in the wilderness. Yet they are important people sent to remind us of difficult but necessary values.

Once each year on Remembrance Sunday, we think of those men and women who during the wars of this century dedicated and lost their lives to protect their country, its citizens, their freedom and rights. We honour their memory with gratitude. It is hard to die for ideals, but very noble. It is often even harder to live for ideals, and never to lose sight of that vision of what is desirable and good. To live for one's ideals requires dedication, and dedication demands selflessness, generosity, courage and tenacity. It must be expressed in deeds and not just in words.

It would be unrealistic to dream of an ideal society, of a Utopia from which all suffering and injustice will have been banished. We must live and work in a world which will always carry the scars of human sin and rebellion. If we dedicate our energies, as we must, to building the kingdom of God in the city of man, then we must be ready to experiment, to renew constantly the structures we have fashioned, to seek new ways of expressing the vision within us. So we need faith and flexibility. We need above all the will to stick to the task and never to be deflected from our purpose by failure or a breakdown in understanding. That is one of the hardest things to do. Only the resolute succeed.

* * * * *

Building the kingdom of God

Jesus Christ gave his Church a mission to the world and to every generation. It is to proclaim the Good News that in Jesus Christ everyone can be reconciled with God and with other people. In every age the same message has to be given: "The kingdom of God is close at hand. Repent and believe the Good News" (Mk 1,15). The proclamation of this Gospel, the call to repentance and our response of faith and conversion are supremely important events both for society and for individuals, and at two levels.

The kingdom of God is everlasting and will be manifest in all its magnificence only at the end of time. Its citizens are adopted as children of God, sharing the divine life and destined for an eternity of union with God. That is one level of reality.

There is a second level. The kingdom of God is also close at hand. Its foundations are being laid here and now in the concrete situations of our daily lives. A new society has to be created for the human race which has been given new dignity and a new future since the Son of God became Son of Mary and died for the sins of his people. In this new society – which is no bigger than a mustard seed and yet is as powerful and pervasive as yeast in dough – men and women affirm their unalienable worth and dignity as individuals. They labour for themselves and others to build "a kingdom of truth and life, a kingdom of holiness and grace, a kingdom of justice, peace and love" (Mass of Christ the King).

If then we repent and believe the Good News, we commit ourselves to the Kingdom in this world as in the next. Through Baptism we are reborn in the likeness of our brother, Jesus Christ. We recognise his likeness in others. We experience a bond between us which transcends differences of gender, race, culture and class. As St Paul says: "All baptised in Christ, you have all clothed yourselves in Christ, and there are no more distinctions between Jew and Greek, slave and free, male and female, but all of you are one in Christ Jesus" (Gal 3,28).

This new-found identity has profound consequences in practice. We can no longer remain indifferent when those who are one with us in Jesus Christ suffer injustice, exploitation and discrimination. We are called to act and to suffer, if necessary, on their behalf. Inevitably this leads to involvement in issues which are usually thought of as social and political. Sometimes, of course, there is little or nothing that can be done, humanly speaking, to change the policies of an oppressive regime or to transform unjust structures. It may be, too, that change can be achieved only at the expense of so much suffering that the cure would be worse than the disease. In such cases, the Christian still has a major contribution to make. It is to learn how to live – and teach others how to live – under such injustice without the sacrifice of integrity and dignity. It involves a deep experience of the Cross and an unshakable hope in the Resurrection.

A call to involvement in social and political issues is often misunderstood and fiercely challenged. Some simply do not see any connection between their personal religious beliefs and their conduct in business, industry and politics. Some stress so strongly the eternal dimension of religion that they seem to regard this world and its affairs as no business of the Church. Others, of course, take a diametrically opposite view and seem to interpret the whole of the gospel in secular and political terms.

The debate on Church and politics is bedevilled from the start by the different senses in which people use either word.

The word 'Church', for example, is used by most to mean the institutional Church and then, specifically, its leadership, Pope, bishops, priests and religious. Only rarely do people remember that Church means also the whole community, the laity as well as the clergy. The claim, for example, that the Church should stay out of politics would make no sense at all if it were to mean that Christians as such are barred from the political process.

There is confusion, too, about the meaning of the word 'politics'. Literally it embraces all that affects the life of people in the city-state. It concerns the management of the affairs of citizens in any local or national community. It has to do with the freedom, prosperity, defence and well-being of all who live in the city of man. Value-systems as well as moral and ethical considerations must obviously have a bearing on politics, understood in this wider sense. It is simply impossible to create a community and regulate the lives and activities of its members in ways which are 'value-free'.

Since religion has to do with people at their deepest level of being and with human relationships as well as with the service of God, it necessarily follows that religion and religious considerations – together with ethical and moral judgments – ought never to be excluded from politics in the wider sense and the affairs of any human community.

There is, of course, a more restricted meaning of the word 'politics'. It is used, particularly in countries like the United Kingdom, to denote the actual functioning of the political process, and the ways whereby vested interests or groups of like-minded citizens achieve their aims. It is applied, for example, to the exercise of power at local or national level, to the organisation and functioning of political parties, to the struggle for domination between conflicting ideologies and political philosophies. It has to do with parties and the cut and thrust of public life. Here, within the unity of the State, sectional interests compete with greater or less freedom, depending on the political complexion of the State. If 'politics' means this, then it is hard to see here a legitimate role for the Church as an institution or for its leadership.

I say 'hard' and not 'impossible' because I would not rule out entirely the possibility of such a role and for limited periods in times of emergency and severe crisis. It would be possible, for example, to justify some political function for the Church when the normal processes of representation have broken down or have been suppressed. It may be necessary in critical situations for the Church to speak and act on behalf of the nation or in the interests of groups unjustly silenced and oppressed. The leaders of the Church may, on occasions, be called on to act as 'honest brokers' or to be the trusted and only possible mediators at times of bitter conflict. All that, however, would be by way of exception. Routine and structured involvement in the political scene is obviously out of character for the institutional Church. Confessional political parties would, in countries like Britain for example, be quite inappropriate, even though the Churches on occasion have to defend their interests and those of their members in the political arena or they have to speak out when human rights and dignity are threatened.

The laity, by contrast, have an inescapable responsibility to involve themselves as citizens of their local and national community. They have a role in party politics as well as in the broader political issues. They choose their party allegiance according to their political philosophy or preferences. They will be found in parties across the political spectrum, yet they should bring to politics the values and ideas they have discovered in the gospel and in the social teachings of the Church. It has to be admitted, of course, that there is no specifically Christian solution to the economic problems of the world, no detailed Christian answer to industrial disputes, and yet the Christian citizen and politician will be guided by some fundamental beliefs about man and society, about human dignity and freedom.

Some Catholics today find these distinctions irksome and unnecessary. They see no difference between the role of the priest and layman in politics. They want the Church as an institution to be committed to the political struggle. This is a complex and hotly disputed question and the arguments are constantly shifting as the situation develops.

The situation in countries round the world differs greatly. It would never be wise to try to lay down hard and fast rules applicable everywhere and for all time about the respective roles of priest and layperson in politics. There are, however, some general principles to guide us. The role of the bishop and the priest as his collaborator is to be 'another Christ', acting in the heart of the Christian community. Bishop and priest are, by definition, men of unity, gathering around themselves the whole people of God. They are meant to reconcile and not be partisan. They carry out in our day the triple role of Christ as priest, prophet and pastor; that is to say, they offer sacrifice and sanctify; they teach, exhort and inspire the people of God; they lead the whole people on the pilgrimage of faith towards the eternal homeland. The layperson finds his or her role principally in those circumstances of everyday life where their life and work place them. As husbands and wives, as parents, as workers or professional people, in local communities and on a wider stage, the laity help to sanctify their surroundings, their families, their workplaces, the communities of which they are members. They do it by the witness of their lives, the silent effect of their presence at the heart of secular life, and by the influence of their words and action aimed at creating a more just and human society. This is the lay vocation: to bring society back to God; to offer it to Him as a living sacrifice of praise. On the other hand, the vocation of the ordained minister is, in the classic phrase beloved of the Christian worker movements, to call, form and sustain the laity in their own proper vocation. It is always a mistake for the laity to allow themselves to be clericalised. It is also a mistake for the clergy to take to themselves tasks proper to the laity. In doing so they 'clericalise' what should be the role of the laity in the world.

The roles of the clergy and the laity are complementary. In practice, both in the world and in the Church community, there may be on occasion some overlapping of responsibilities, but the broad distinction of function should remain intact. If the priest who should represent the principle of reconciliation and unity in the community becomes too directly and personally involved in the political process, he runs the risk of dividing his community and unnecessarily antagonising some of its members. His public stance on political matters which should properly be left to the initiative and concern of the laity may have the effect of driving some people out of the Church in anger and protest.

Although critics claim that the Church these days is over-political, experience would indicate that Christians in general are not as yet inspired by the demands of the Gospel. Clergy and laity, in their different ways, face an uphill   task. There are issues of human rights and freedoms under Communist regimes and in black Africa, as well as in more publicised countries of Central and Latin America and in South Africa. There is an almost universal need to protect and defend what is human against attacks from many quarters. Here the Christian must be ready to publicise, to protest and to exert pressure in whatever way is appropriate. It is also necessary to uphold the moral law and to denounce wickedness in all its forms. It is crucial and difficult in the climate of society today to defend the right to life, to uphold public and private integrity and honesty, to resist the easy recourse to falsehood in every walk of life. And the Church must seek in every possible way to care for the poor, the handicapped and the unfortunate. In a society which is becoming more unfeeling it is necessary for the Christian to speak up for the inarticulate and the powerless, to engage public sympathy for those in distress and to contribute materially to the relief of those in need.

The bishop and the priest will have a role to play as important as the lay Christian's, but different. Even in a democratic and free society it is often necessary for them to take the lead in rousing public opinion and in educating people on the issues of justice and peace. They can speak, write and teach. They encourage the laity and support them in their proper task. For then it is the role of the laity with their experience and expertise to fashion ways of their own choosing to translate their Christian ideals and principles into effective action. They are the ones with free access to political parties and pressure groups. It is entirely their task to see that things happen. And they must.

The Christian contribution to all such practical action in the world must spring from the deepest and purest springs of the Christian life. Bishops, priests and laity alike are not simply humanitarian. Whatever they do should be motivated by a Christian love of God and neighbour. If I involve myself in building the kingdom of God on earth that is entirely consistent with my pursuit of the eternal. When Jesus Christ spoke of judgment day in Matthew 25,31–46, he portrayed the King as concerned solely with the way people had treated each other in their life-time. Had they fed the hungry, given drink to the thirsty, welcomed the stranger, clothed the naked, visited the sick and the imprisoned? Their actions were judged to have been directed towards the Son of Man himself, to the person of Jesus Christ. In him, true God and true man, heaven and earth meet and believers discover how to make sense of their daily tasks in this life and their longing for ultimate union with God in heaven. They learn how to balance the temporal and the eternal.

If I am in the market place serving Christ in my brothers and sisters, there is part of me longing to be in the desert, alone with God. When I am in the desert alone with Him, there is a part of me eager to rush back to the market place to be with the others. When we try to live both these commandments, loving God and our neighbour, we discover that the two become one. We cannot love God or mankind unless we learn about God from our experience of others and learn to love others in the light of our commitment to God and His Son, Jesus Christ.

Loving God must indeed include loving those made in His image and likeness. Loving my neighbour leads me to discover in them the face of the Father's Divine Son. The face of Christ will be seen in a quite special manner in those who are bruised and who suffer. This is why active concern for our neighbour is an essential element of our spiritual lives and our religious growth.

The twin commandment has to become a single inspiration. It must drive me to build the kingdom of God on earth. It must leave me longing for the heavenly Jerusalem.

*   *   *   *   *

A better world

The glory of God is present in the marvels of our world. There is beauty to please the eye and the ear. There is genius to be admired in the skill of the human mind as it probes the secrets hidden within reality, as it harnesses and controls the great powers latent within the universe. We can adore God as the maker of all things; we can transform humanity's inventions and skills into hymns of praise. To do this we need to recognise whence comes creation and all the gifts we use and what is the ultimate purpose of our endeavours.

We have the power to do these things, but have we the will? Have we the will to heal ourselves, recover wholeness, so that our priorities are right? Is it possible to build a better world? I think it is certainly possible to make progress. Human beings have the potential to live lives which are richer, more fulfilled, more secure. That can happen even though there will always be some frustration and failure.

* * *

My deepest conviction is that the ultimate answers can be found only in Jesus Christ and in his Gospel, and the conversion he came to preach. Unless we learn to die to ourselves and to live for God, all our striving may remain a cunningly concealed struggle for power and domination. We may seek to reform, and find we have only succeeded in shifting the balance of power without reducing the sum of human misery.

Our present day confusion and the lack of unity within the State, within secular society, reveal the need for discovering a common vision, an agreed understanding about the nature, the dignity and the rights of man. This will be impossible without a recognition of the spiritual dimension in each individual, and without acknowledgment of the eternal, the divine. We need to rekindle a sense of religion in our people. The great monotheistic religions represented in our society today, the Christian, Jewish and Muslim could each make their distinctive contribution. There is need for a national dialogue of faith.

It can hardly be denied that as a nation we have lost our religious sense. As a consequence we are experiencing a dulling of our moral sense. Legitimate freedoms are being menaced by increasing licence. I am not advocating a return to Victorian values, since not all these were by any means profoundly religious or moral. But there is an obvious need for greater self-discipline, for unselfishness, for self-control to curb greed, indulgence, cruelty and carelessness over others' rights. Nobody is naturally thoughtful, generous and tolerant. There is need for training, for discipline, for example, and social support.

Our society needs the bond of a common purpose, of tasks freely agreed on and pursued with vigour by different interest groups. There is so much to do, and perhaps not much time left. The Brandt Report on World Development warned us that there is a world crisis, that there is no guarantee that it can be contained and that urgent action is required.

Can we not find common ground in recognising that there must be respect in our society for every person simply as a person? All of us must come to acknowledge that the person is primary and not society. The State exists for people, not people for the State.

* * * * *

Renew the face of the earth

There are two significant images from the Bible with profound implications for Catholics today. Both of them are about beginnings. Both of them lead us into the mystery of God and the mystery of His saving love for the universe He created and for mankind made in His image and likeness. One is from the Book of Genesis in the Old Testament, the other from the Gospel of St Luke in the New Testament. Both will tell us much about the reality of the Holy Spirit.

The Book of Genesis sets out in a series of images a primitive but vivid account of how the world came into being. Across many centuries the poetry speaks to us today:

> "In the beginning,
>   God created the heavens and the earth.
>   Now the earth was a formless void,
>   there was darkness over the deep,
>   and God's spirit hovered over the water" (Gen 1,1)

In the darkness there is the primaeval chaos, the swirling waters and the brooding power of God. The image suggests infinite creativity, perhaps even the fleeting suggestion of a giant bird hatching its young. But we are left with a vision of infinite love drawing out of emptiness the beauty of the world, the glory of the heavens, the form and order of all created things. For centuries men and women have been enriched and encouraged by this fundamental image. It has helped them to recognise God as creator, as Father. Even today it helps us to make sense of our experience and of the world around us.

The second image is to be found in St Luke's account of the beginning of the public ministry of Jesus. He had come, after forty days of fasting in the desert, to his home town of Nazareth. On the Sabbath, in the Synagogue, he was handed the scroll of Isaiah to read. The words proclaimed were:

"The spirit of the Lord has been given to me,
for he has anointed me.
He has sent me to bring the good news to the poor,
to proclaim liberty to captives,
to the blind new sight,
to set the downtrodden free,
to proclaim the Lord's year of freedom" (Is 61,1–2)

Then he said: "This text is being fulfilled today even as you listen". Luke had previously described how John had baptised Jesus in the waters of the Jordan and the Holy Spirit had descended on him like a dove. There are indications here surely of a new creation. The Spirit of God hovers over the water. A new Adam steps from the Jordan and proclaims to the people that a new hope and a new liberation has been given to them. It has been given in particular to the poor, the captive, the blind and the downtrodden.

Jesus Christ walked the length and breadth of Galilee and Judea. Wherever he went he brought health and wholeness, peace and healing, forgiveness and new life. The power of God and the Spirit of God renewed through him the face of the earth. This is still our mission and the mission of the Church. It is a mission today of immense complexity and difficulty.

Deep in the heart of mankind, and enshrined in the structures of our world society, is a selfishness and a greed inherited from the first Adam, the first Eve. We, the fallen and sinful, struggle to secure what we want, regardless of others. We who are blind and deaf to the promptings of God's Spirit have built for ourselves a world that is unjust, a world of hunger, of malnutrition and despair. The poverty of the third world, the unemployment and inequalities of the industrialised West, are the grim face of our rejection of God, of our rebellion against the Spirit of God.

Slowly, painfully, we seek to allow the Spirit of God to renew the face of the earth. The restoration of society can only be achieved by those who are poor in spirit, gentle, compassionate, hungry for justice, merciful, pure in heart, and peacemakers. Only those who are part of the new creation can hope to build a new world, a better society. The kingdom of God is established first in our hearts. Unless that happens our efforts will remain generous and well-intentioned but not the work of the Holy Spirit.

The Spirit of God fashioned our world. The Spirit of God restored our fallen world in Jesus Christ. It is our mission, throughout our lives to share the work of Christ and to renew, through the power of the Spirit, the face of the earth.

*   *   *   *   *

The Church in the modern world

We are being called to become a new people, a people whose hearts have been converted and who seek new heavens and a new earth. For my own part, I turn constantly to two great images in the New Testament. The first is the story of Dives and Lazarus in Luke ch. 16: the rich man at his table, the beggar at the gate. The terrifying judgment on the rich man, Dives, seems to be God's verdict on the 'haves' and the 'have-nots'. The 'haves' are condemned for indifference to their fellow-men and for enjoying the good life while others starved.

The other image is that of the final judgment given to us in Matthew ch. 25. We shall be judged and rewarded if we have fed the hungry, given drink to the thirsty, clothed the naked, welcomed the stranger, visited the prisoners and the sick. I have always taken that to demand of me more than almsgiving. It is not enough to scatter crumbs from the rich man's table; we must provide the poor with soil and seed and the security of a harvest.

Surely the message of Jesus Christ to us is that we are always to identify with others, to offer them solidarity and service. Our fellow feeling drives us to imitate Christ at the Last Supper, girding ourselves with a towel, getting down to the lowliest of jobs, content to honour and serve our brothers and sisters, respecting their dignity while meeting their needs. That commitment to service is not just personal; it must involve the whole Church, all who are followers of Christ. As individuals and as the Church, we have to give ourselves, our time, our energies, our labour, both to God and to our fellow men. It is the basic inspiration for the Church's commitment to society and to others.

It is sometimes hard to see the present for what it is. I believe that the Second Vatican Council has helped us to make sense of our Christian vocation today. The Council gave us, among other things, a charter for Catholic laity. In the Constitution on the Church (Lumen Gentium) the rightful place of the laity in the Church was recognised, and their programme for action in the world was set out in the document called 'The Church in the Modern World' (Gaudium et Spes).

In the past the Church's social teaching has had a profound effect on the Christian formation of generations of Catholics. This was in large measure the work of apostolic lay organisations. It resulted in many Catholics becoming involved in local and national politics, in public and civic life. It meant that some Catholics also became deeply committed to working for international justice and peace and to defending human rights throughout the world.

Catholic social teaching is not as well-known today as it should be. If it were better known, Catholics would be more encouraged to become actively involved in their local communities, in political life and in trade unions and professional organisations.

When we set out to seek the kingdom of God, to build a better world, we must be ready to face criticisms. Some of these criticisms will be based on misunderstandings. Some say, without any qualification at all, "The Church should keep out of politics". Certainly the bishops and priests of the Church should never meddle in party politics.

Certainly the leadership of the Church should not be

identified with one particular party, nor should it inter-
fere with the legitimate freedom of the voter. But so
many political questions are moral issues and affect the
rights and the well-being of individuals or sections of
the community. Bishops and priests have to be involved
when it is a question of morality and human dignity and
rights.

It is vital to remember that the laity too are the
Church. It is their most serious obligation to involve
themselves in their own world of work, social concerns
and politics. Here they act in accordance with their
conscience. They choose their political allegiance. In
the real world of affairs, there is not usually one simple
Christian solution. There are Christian values all would
share but Christians come to different conclusions as
they apply their principles to political, social and
industrial problems. Catholics should belong to different
parties. They should be involved in trade unions. They
should take their rightful place at every level of public
life and service. They should be united in their loyalty
to Christ and to the values of the Gospel and their sense
of Christian brotherhood.

Some say that fewer Catholics than before are involved
in politics, trade unions, local government. Certainly
there are fewer in the apostolic lay organisations and
movements. Perhaps the reason may be found in the
fact that since the Second Vatican Council, many
committed Catholics have devoted themselves to the
renewal of the Church itself. They have been active in
parish councils, commissions, special ministries and
other works of great value to the Church. It may however have distracted them from their responsibility to
be witnessing Christians in the modern world.

*   *   *

There are those who would argue that it is the task of
Church leaders and of her corporate membership to be
active - even sometimes violent - in the struggle for

justice and peace, to set about the practical reform of structural injustice at home and abroad and to be politically involved at every level with bringing about a new social order. They should not, in this view, be afraid to work alongside others with different convictions; they should feel free to adopt concepts and techniques from alien systems. The opposite view would hold that the Church's only concern is with souls and with the eternal destiny of men and women. In this view the Church would be confined to an exclusively spiritual role.

Neither view is a balanced one. The Church can never be the servant of an ideology or of a political system, nor can she be exclusively concerned with the next world. Pope John Paul II gave us all guidance in his authoritative statement to the Latin American bishops at Puebla in January 1979. He said this:

> "If the Church makes herself present in the defence of or in the advancement of man, she does so in line with her mission, which although it is religious and not social and political, cannot fail to consider man in the entirety of his being... She does not have to have recourse to ideological systems in order to love, defend and collaborate in the liberation of man; at the centre of the message of which she is the depository and herald, she finds inspiration for acting in favour of brotherhood, justice and peace, against all forms of domination, slavery, discrimination, violence, attacks on religious liberty and aggression against man and whatever attacks life. The Church wishes to stay free with regard to competing systems in order to opt only for man. Whatever the miseries of sufferings that afflict man, it is not through violence, the interplay of power and political systems, but through the truth concerning man that he journeys towards a better future".

It is not for the Church as a whole to advocate this or that political constitution. It is not for her spiritual leaders to pronounce on the best monetary policy or economic system. Instead she is concerned with something deeper and more far-reaching. She is the guardian of a priceless treasure since she is principally engaged with "the truth concerning man". In accordance with her prophetic role, she has to ensure, as far as she can, that the spiritual good of every individual is safeguarded and that people are made free to grow to their full stature. She knows that neither objective can be achieved if individuals and societies ignore or defy the law of God. She knows, too, that she must be ready for vigorous action and public witness. Men and women need both vision and hope if they are to set about building the kingdom of God. That vision and hope are given to them by God's revelation.

*   *   *   *   *

National values

When Queen Elizabeth acceded to the throne, she asked in a very special manner that her subjects should pray for her, and the celebration of her Jubilee twenty-five years later became an unusually intense display of the respect and affection the nation feels for her and her family. I have vivid memories of the celebration.

Before going to St Paul's Cathedral I wandered through the streets where people were gathering round Buckingham Palace. I think that in those two experiences – mingling with the crowd and then the more solemn occasion at St Paul's – were two aspects of the celebrations so characteristic of our nation at its best. There was the sense of friendship, of joy, of good humour in the streets, and then the solemn turning to God. In St Paul's there was tangibly an atmosphere of prayer, a sense of wanting to say 'thank you' to God.

I believe that the spontaneous response to the Jubilee took many people by surprise. Perhaps there were some who thought that kind of celebration was no longer important, in the sense that perhaps our nation had grown cold, and worse still, possibly a little cynical. Yet, people were taken by surprise because the ordinary person sensed the importance of the occasion and, however confusedly, experienced in it the presence of God.

The Jubilee proved to be a symbol of many values which had seemed in danger of eclipse. In the first place it stressed love of our country. That is not an outworn or irrelevant value. If we fail to love our country, what is there left to honour and revere? To love one's country is a virtue. Without honourable patriotism, how can one learn to give proper honour and respect to other countries and their peoples? Again, whatever divisions there are in our land, however controversial certain issues are in our society, nonetheless we can still find ourselves at one; we are one nation. The Jubilee gave us an opportunity to halt for a day the ordinary round of our everyday existence and gave us the chance to reflect on what it means to be part of this complex and vast community which is modern Britain. We have deep roots in a shared past; we face together common problems, dangers and opportunities; we need firm resolve to match the challenge of the future. If we cannot forge common values and shared loyalties our society will suffer. All that, I believe, lay behind the simple rejoicing on Jubilee day.

For myself there was one moment to be relished above all others and one which seemed to me, not only to sum up what the Jubilee meant, but to give guidance to what the nation requires. It was to be found in the last words of Her Majesty's speech at the Guildhall:

> "When I was twenty one, I pledged my life to the service of my people and I asked God's help to make good that vow. Although that vow was made in my salad days when I was green in judgment, I do not regret or retract one word of it".

Here was the central point of all the celebrations. By

those words we were reminded that in youth we can pledge ourselves to good and to God and can be true to that pledge; that we can pledge ourselves to each other and be true to that promise. In later years we can pause and renew that pledge to good and to God.

We must emphasise this becaue it is important for ordinary people from every walk of life. People everywhere need something to lift up their lives, to give them real point and meaning. The Queen's pledge can be echoed by ordinary people everywhere. It was the important people who misjudged just how much the celebrations would grip the imagination of the ordinary people who took over. This suggests just how much power there is in the hands of ordinary decent people when they are seized by a vision, however dimly perceived.

In every aspect of our national life, their voice should be heard, the values they still hold dear should prevail.

The issues

Forces of unbelief

The individual pilgrim and the whole pilgrim Church cannot pass through the world untouched and unscathed by what surrounds them. Our times and our world are shaped by us under the providence of the Lord of history. We bear an inescapable responsibility for our own society and for the environment in which we live. We are ambassadors of Christ and his Gospel. We must be conscious of the dangers we face without being overwhelmed or paralysed by them.

Atheism and humanism – the forces of unbelief – are well-known enemies of the Gospel. They pose a different threat in Eastern Europe and in the West. In the West they seep insidiously into society; they threaten to undermine its foundations. The mass media provide their proponents with access to every home. An atmosphere of secularism is gradually but effectively created. It then becomes difficult to counter, as we must, this spirit of our age. In Eastern Europe, on the other hand, atheism poses a more aggressive threat and motivates the policies of state institutions. For more than thirty years, atheistic communism has imposed grave restrictions on religious freedom. While it may tolerate public worship, it demands public support of the regime and its policies and it restricts severely the independent expression of religious opinion, the possibility of presenting the religious case in public and the freedom of the Church to educate and form the young in the Christian faith.

It is a stark fact that many countries today experience widespread de-christianisation. People may have been baptised, but in practice they live quite outside the Christian Church. We must learn somehow to preach to those who by baptism are Christians but who by knowledge of their religion and style of life most decidedly are not. How do we approach the well-educated who have rejected Christianity as irrelevant to their lives?

The lapsed, the non-practising, present us with a complex task. There are many degrees and kinds of lapsation. The late Pope Paul VI once wrote: "The phenomenon of the non-practising is a very ancient one in the history of Christianity; it is the result of a natural weakness, a profound inconsistency which we, unfortunately, bear deep within us. Today, however, it shows certain new characteristics. It is often the result of the uprooting typical of our time. It also springs from the fact that Christians live in close proximity with non-believers and consequently experience the effects of unbelief. Furthermore, the non-practising Christians of today, more so than those of previous periods, seek to explain and justify their position in the name of an interior religion, of personal independence or authenticity" (Evangelii Nuntiandi n. 56). There can be no doubt that the number of non-practising Christians grows alarmingly. In Britain, less than 10% of the total population go to church on Sunday. The number of Catholics who attend Sunday Mass each week is slowly declining. We must find ways to reverse this. Part of the problem is that many of our Catholics have received the sacraments, however infrequently, but have never been brought to the point of making a personal commitment to Christ. As we sometimes express it, too many people have been 'sacramentalised' but not 'evangelised'. We cannot ignore the problem they present.

Nor can we neglect the task of deepening and supporting the faith of all believers. We cannot take for granted their faithfulness and perseverance in such adverse situations. What is needed is not evangelisation in the strict sense of a first proclamation of the Gospel, but a more vigorous catechesis so radical and so sustained that it might be called a continuing evangelisation. We must constantly challenge the faithful – including ourselves – with the person and message of Jesus Christ, with the fulness of the Word of God. Faith has to be deepened, strengthened, made more mature. As the Synod of 1977 recognised, this means that we must create programmes of catechesis for adults. This is "the principal form of catechesis because it is addressed to persons who have the greatest responsibilities and the capacity to live the Christian message in its fully developed form" (Catechesi Tradendae n. 43).

* * * * *

War and peace

War, indiscriminate destruction, the deliberate recourse to terrorism in pursuit of political aims constitute formidable barriers to the preaching of Christ's Gospel in our day. The Church tries to preach love, reconciliation and universal brotherhood in a sinful world where individuals and states use aggression and violence to secure their purposes.

The Christian vision of peace is of a different order from the secular world's understanding. Peace is not simply an absence of armed hostilities. The Church has been mandated by Christ to bring his peace to the world: "Peace I bequeath to you, my own peace I give you, a peace the world cannot give" (Jn 14,27). St Paul teaches us that Jesus Christ himself is our peace, who overcomes the divisiveness of man's sinfulness by reconciling the world to God and restoring unity among the peoples (cf. Eph 2,13–18).

The biblical and Christian concept of peace is bound up necessarily with the ideals of righteousness and justice – with honouring one's responsibilities to God and to one's neighbour. In the New Testament there is the revelation of God's saving love for us and the new commandment that we are to love others as Christ loves them (cf. Jn 13,34). Here we come to the heart of the new covenant and to the Gospel of peace. We must be heralds of reconciliation and that means we must be peacemakers. Those who preach the Gospel must work to establish the kingdom among men. It means that the Church and the individual Christian are committed to reconcile those at variance, to heal those injustices and inequalities that breed bitterness and conflict, to witness at all times to the brotherhood of man. We have to bring to the world Christ, its peace. We must work for that conversion of heart which is the necessary condition for peace. We have to try to construct a society where war is unthinkable.

Here the Christian ideal might seem out of touch with reality. History points to persistent failure and would seem to prove that war is inevitable. In contrast to such pessimism, John XXIII, Paul VI and John Paul II have repeatedly asserted that peace is possible, that peace is necessary. A new awareness of the horrors of war is beginning to haunt the consciousness of the world. War has changed its nature. No longer is it waged between professional armies. No longer is it limited in its effects and in its toll of human life. Conventional as well as nuclear weapons now assume an awesome power. Individual Christians and the Christian Church are now beginning to face the moral implications of the new world picture. For centuries it seemed that the classical 'just war' tradition was sufficient guide for the Christian conscience. Now it would seem that the Church's most urgent priority is a crusade for peace – a crusade which is not political, but part of its evangelising mission.

Here I can see a new and important role for the Church in Europe. In 1982 I was at a meeting with about eighty bishops at a symposium in Rome which was concerned with our shared responsibility for evangelising the whole continent. The bishops came from East and West, from the Atlantic to the Urals, from

Scandinavia to Malta. There was brotherhood, communion and a common purpose. We were undivided in a
divided continent. We represented local churches of
believers who already belong to a community of reconciliation. I realised then how powerful could be our
influence to help heal the wounds of division in our
continent. We can be an important voice urging restraint,
understanding and peace. We can use our abilities and
resources to build bridges between unreconciled neighbours. We can help to reduce tension and to build
confidence. We can play a major part in educating our
own congregations and our children in the ways of
peace. That is surely a way forward for our Church in
future.

At other times and in other places I have tried to
wrestle with the complex problem of the morality of
nuclear deterrence. Here, reflecting only on the fundamental attitudes of the Christian pilgrim, I would want
to stress above all that the pilgrim should long for the
peace of Christ, should pray for it, should work and
struggle for it. The whole Church struggles to remain
sane in a mad world. We do not advocate in any sense
the recourse to violence and war. Some Christians
with the greatest reluctance and regret will admit that,
in our fallen world, force may sometimes have to be
used as a last resort in defence of fundamental freedoms
and human rights. They would lay down the most
stringent conditions. They urge unceasing effort to
limit the destructiveness of human conflict. They hold
out continually to the world the Christian ideal of
peace and universal brotherhood. The policy of nuclear
deterrence provides the human race with no assurances
for the future.

My nightmare is that man will undo at the end of
time what God had created in the beginning. I fear that
the human story which began with Genesis may end
with a fearful chapter given over to Nemesis. Will we
have to endure the return of God's world to that primaeval chaos from which it emerged? Intellectually
I can accept that the policy of deterrence is morally

defensible, but only on the understanding that it must be no more than a stage towards multilateral and total disarmament. Nonetheless, everything Christian and human within me cries out in protest against the sheer horror of a world where these weapons are allowed to exist at all.

*   *   *   *   *

Christian disunity

There can be no doubt that a major obstacle to the effectiveness and well-being of the pilgrim people of God is disunity in its ranks. Pope Paul VI once asked whether this was not one of the great sicknesses of evangelisation today (Evangelii Nuntiandi n. 77). Throughout this century it has become clear that, moved by the Spirit of God, Christians have experienced increasing frustration and impatience with divisions among themselves. Non-believers, too, readily take refuge in criticism of Christian disharmony. It is easy to be discouraged at the pace of our progress. I believe it helps instead to look over our shoulders and to marvel at the ground we have already covered.

Those brought up in the rigidity and religious isolation of the 1930's and 40's have now to adapt themselves to a new climate of respect and collaboration among the Churches. During his visit to Britain in 1982, Pope John Paul II signed a Common Declaration with Dr Runcie, the Archbishop of Canterbury. It contained these remarkable words: "Our aim is not limited to the union of our two Communions alone, to the exclusion of other Christians, but rather extends to the fulfilment of God's will for the visible unity of all His people. Both in our present dialogue and in those engaged in by other

Christians among themselves and with us, we recognise in the agreements we are able to reach, as well as in the difficulties which we encounter, a renewed challenge to abandon ourselves completely to the truth of the Gospel". It is only by abandoning ourselves completely to the truth of the Gospel that all our Christian divisions can be overcome and the way to Christian unity can be pursued humbly and yet with utter confidence. Our divisions must not hinder any longer the urgent need for Christians to preach together the Gospel of Jesus Christ.

*   *   *   *   *

Ecumenism: some thoughts

We Christians have reached a stage in our journey together when we will have to face honestly and courageously the obstacles which lie ahead, and there are many unresolved questions between us all. Roman Catholics in particular would want to make progress in three particular areas. Some of these problems have been tackled in conversation between ourselves and other Christian Churches. But we need more prayer, study and dialogue on the role of the Pope, on the role and mission of the bishops, and on the sacraments. What we have already been given is a new context, a new perspective.

When the Bishop of Rome recently came to Britain he visited his own people to pray with them, to administer the Sacraments, to confirm their faith. That much was expected. What was totally surprising was that this Bishop of Rome made solemn and significant visits to the Anglican Cathedrals of Canterbury and Liverpool. The prolonged applause of the people as the Pope entered the cathedrals, and the expression on their faces, were in themselves an appeal to God for the precious gift of unity. Furthermore, he held conversations with other Church leaders and invited them to Rome to continue talks. Wherever the Pope went he spoke of his deep concern to recover unity among Christians. It was more than conventional courtesy. Only recently in Rome he has spoken of Britain as a "special ecumenical terrain".

Should this astonish anyone? In his concern for unity John Paul II continues a venerable tradition of the Roman See. As a matter of history, the prestige, the authority of the Roman See in its universal aspect, deepened and expanded as it was seen to fulfil a mission of unity for the whole Church. The See of Rome was seen to guide that communion in faith and life which belonged to every Church where the apostolic faith was preached and maintained.

The primacy is for unity. Rightly understood, it implies that the Bishop of Rome exercises his oversight in order to guard and promote the fidelity of all the Churches to Christ and to one another. Communion with him is intended as a safeguard of the catholicity of each local Church, it is a sign of the communion of all the Churches.

The Anglican/Roman Catholic International Commission has agonised for more than five years over the Papacy and over the complex problem of how it is related to the position of Peter, freely recognised in the New Testament, and the same enquiry must be undertaken with each Church as we progress towards unity.

Pope Paul VI once said: "The Pope, as you well know, is undoubtedly the gravest obstacle in the path of ecumenism". It should be our task as Roman Catholics to show that the successor of Peter, far from being an obstacle to unity, is in fact an indispensable means of achieving it. We believe that the authority of the Pope has been divinely ordained as the way to preserve "truth, charity and unity" among Christians. At the same time we Catholics have to remind ourselves, when we take our stand on papal authority as continuing the ministry of Peter, that we do not claim that this entails a total and uncritical acceptance of any specific style of Church government at any given moment in history. We must not confuse what is essential with what is relative. Furthermore, the Pope's universal ministry is not something separate from the ministry of the Church. It does not pursue some purpose different from that of the Church. It relates to the unity of the whole flock, as the Bishop relates to the unity of his own local Church, and has done from early times.

It was remarkable how much courtesy and respect Pope John Paul showed for the Ministers of all the Churches he encountered during his visit. I hope that there will be resolute efforts to tackle the obstacles to mutual recognition of ministries in the spirit of the Common Declaration signed by Pope John Paul II and Archbishop Runcie at Canterbury. The Anglican/Roman Catholic International Commission laid down the principle that "agreement on the nature of ministry is prior to the consideration of the mutual recognition of ministries". That study, which is being pursued in so many other dialogues besides the Anglican/Roman Catholic one, must now be pursued with renewed vigour.

Reconciliation of ministries cannot be cheaply bought, or sought for simple convenience. The process of reconciling ministries will be long and arduous. We should not allow that to obscure the fact that graces have been given down the ages through the ministers of the different Churches. Furthermore, all of us need to go back and enter profoundly into the great tradition of the undivided Church. Insularity does not come merely from living on an island. There is a kind of insularity of time which can afflict us all if we consider only those parts of history which suit us.

The sacraments are part of that heritage from the undivided Church. One reason why the Pope's visit attracted and impressed people beyond the confines of the Roman Catholic community was that he was seen in action at the heart of the Church's life, administering the sacraments. The great sacrament, the Eucharist, has been at the centre of ecumenical discussion from the beginning. So too has Baptism. The central importance of the sacramental principle led the Second Vatican Council to begin its Constitution on the Church by describing the Church itself as a "kind of sacrament or sign of intimate union with God, and of the unity of all mankind. She is also an instrument for the achievement of such union and unity". The Council's Constitution on the Liturgy stresses even more strikingly the all-pervading nature of the sacramental principle when it says that the "liturgy of the sacraments and sacramentals sanctifies almost every event in the lives of the faithful . . .". A growing convergence among the Churches in acknowledging the deep human and deep theological significance of the sacramental principle will be a powerful force in our movement towards unity. It is illustrated by the Lima Agreement on Baptism, Eucharist and Ministry which represents a convergence among all the major Churches of the world.

I am convinced that these three themes – Peter, apostolicity and sacraments – are themes which in one way or another all the Churches are now talking about. They are part of the whole plan of human salvation. They are the ways in which we who live at the close of the twentieth century can be in living touch with the teaching, the redeeming work, the very life of Jesus who is the way, the truth and the life.

*   *   *   *   *

The hungry world

When the bishops of the Church at the Second Vatican Council reflected on the role of the Church in the modern world they completed their consideration of war and peace and then turned immediately to the rich and poor nations. They taught: "If peace is to be established the first condition is to root out the causes of discord among men which lead to wars – in the first place, injustice. Not a few of these causes arise out of excessive economic inequalities and out of hesitation to undertake necessary corrections. Some are due to the desire for power and to contempt for people, and at a deeper level, to envy, distrust and other selfish passions" (GS 83). Or again, in the words of Pope Paul in 'Populorum Progressio': "Development is the new name for peace". The crisis of possessions, like the crisis of power, is intimately connected with human sinfulness and thus with the Church's mission of evangelisation and with the gospel of reconciliation. It, too, is therefore a proper subject for Christian reflection, concern and action.

I want to make three comments: first, that the Church's appreciation of the issues of poverty, social inequality and structural injustice, like its understanding of war and peace, is deepening and developing at this present time; secondly, that the Church now sees the development of peoples as embracing every aspect of human life and not simply as a matter of economics; thirdly, that justice is a constitutive element of the Gospel, and that the pursuit of justice lies at the heart of the Church's mission.

In the past Christians responded to inequalities in the social order and to grievous deprivation and poverty by giving generously to charity and by involving themselves in countless 'works of mercy'. Gradually there has dawned the realisation that alleviation of the symptoms of a sick world is not enough; the causes have to be removed. The Synod of Bishops in 1971 pointed out that in the Old Testament, God reveals Himself to us as liberator of the oppressed and the defender of the poor, demanding from man faith in Him and justice towards man's neighbour. It is only in the observance of the duties of justice that God is truly recognised as the liberator of the oppressed (Justice in the World, ch. 2).

Jesus Christ proclaimed the fatherhood of God towards all men and the intervention of God's justice on behalf of the needy and the oppressed (Lk 6,20–23). In this way he identified himself with his 'least brethren' as he stated: "As you did it to one of the least of my brethren, you did it to me" (Mt 25,40). The bishops teach that man's relationship to his neighbour is bound up with his relationship to God; his response to the love of God, saving us through Christ, is shown to be effective in his love and service of men. Love implies a recognition of the dignity and rights of one's neighbour. Justice attains its inner fulness only in love. Because every man is truly a visible image of the invisible God and a brother of Christ, the Christian finds in every man God himself and God's absolute demand for justice and love (Justice in the World, ch. 2 passim). There are here signs of a real development of teaching in the Church.

Secondly, every individual has a right not only to life itself but to genuine human growth. This was expressed vividly by Pope Paul VI in his encyclical, 'Populorum Progressio'. In the passage headed 'The Christian Vision of Development', the Pope explained: "Development cannot be limited to mere economic growth. In order to be authentic, it must be complete, integral, that is, it has to promote the good of every man and of the whole man . . . In the design of God, every man is called upon to develop and fulfil himself, for every life is a vocation . . . This self-fulfilment is not something optional. Just as the whole of creation is ordained to its Creator, so spiritual beings should, of their own accord, orientate their lives to God, the first truth and supreme good . . . But each man is a member of society. He is part of the whole of mankind. It is not just certain individuals, but all men who are called to this fulness of development. As Christians we must be content with nothing less than a new creation and a new man".

My third and final comment is that the demands of

justice are at the heart of the Gospel. May I quote
again the much-quoted words of the 1971 Synod of
Bishops: "Action on behalf of justice and participation
in the transformation of the world fully appear to us as
a constitutive dimension of the preaching of the Gospel,
or, in other words, of the Church's mission for the
redemption of the human race and its liberation from
every oppressive situation" (Justice in the World,
Introduction). Here, I think, we need to create within
Catholic communities a new awareness. They have been
brought up, as I already said, in a tradition of almsgiving and voluntary aid. They need to open their
eyes to a broader horizon. We all need to reflect on our
human solidarity, within Europe and outside. We need
to see the unbreakable connection between love of God
and love of our neighbour. Again, as with peace and
war, the difficulties seem insurmountable. The world's
anarchy and greed seem unconquerable. The Christian
can never despair and never retreat from the world,
leaving it to its own devices. We go forward hoping in
Christ: "because God wanted all perfection to be found
in him and all things to be reconciled through him and
for him, everything in heaven and everything on earth,
when he made peace by his death on the cross" (Col 1,
19–20).

The Pilgrims

There is no such thing as an 'ordinary Catholic', that is, if we look at what St Peter wrote: "You are a chosen race, a royal priesthood, a consecrated nation, a people God means to have for Himself" (1 Pet 2,9). We should look, too, at the prayer that is said by the celebrant after Baptism when the candidate is anointed with sacred Chrism:

> "God, the Father of Our Lord Jesus Christ, has freed you from all sin, given you a new birth by water and the Holy Spirit, and welcomed you into His holy people. He now anoints you with the chrism of salvation. As Christ was anointed priest, prophet and king, so may you live always as a member of his body sharing everlasting life".

Each baptised person is anointed, as Christ was, priest, prophet and king. In the body of Christ, which is the Church, the baptised person shares in this threefold function of the Head of the body.

The 'ordinary Catholic' - if the phrase has to be used - has then a remarkable dignity. This baby, just baptised, is in some wonderful manner, priest, prophet and king; this lapsed Catholic who has strayed far from the Church, cannot cease to be priest, prophet and king.

We think, increasingly and rightly, about the role of the laity in the Church today. The foundation for this is Baptism. The new Code of Canon Law sums up, in canon 204, the teaching of the Second Vatican Council concerning the laity. It says:

> "Christ's faithful are those who, since they are incorporated into Christ through Baptism, are constituted the people of God. For this reason they participate in their own way in

the priestly, prophetic and kingly office of Christ. They are called, each according to his or her particular condition, to exercise the mission which God entrusted to the Church to fulfil in the world".

*   *   *   *   *

We are priests

The whole Church at different levels is concerned with fulfilling its priestly mission.

This is not the place to explore the full extent of this priestly role. Fundamental is the offering by the people of the sacrifice of their own lives. This is expressed in the communal celebration of the Eucharist, the re-presenting to God of Christ's sacrifice which reconciles man to God. That adoration, thanksgiving and intercession offered by the whole people of God is, when properly understood, of the most profound importance to the human family. It creates and expresses community. It bridges the abyss between God and man. It reconciles man to man in a communal meal which is both a sacrifice and a healing.

The priesthood of the baptised goes further. It finds expression also in the signs and symbols of the sacraments which sanctify the major moments and experiences of life. In this way, the Christian explores and intensifies the deeper experience of what it means to be human. Again, there is the daily personal relationship with God which exists through prayer and is nourished by it. Here once more the baptised, as priests, represent the whole of mankind when they pray; through Christ, with Christ and in Christ they offer prayer, praise and constant intercession for the needs of themselves and their neighbours.

Perhaps unfashionably, in an age of social concern and action, I would claim that the priestly role of the Christian and of the whole people of God is the most essential for the coherence of our society, for its well-being and for its spiritual and psychic health. Uprooted and superficial as we have become individually, we have lost, too, our sense of identity with each other in community. The priesthood of each Christian, consciously embraced, can serve to restore awareness of the transcendent and a sense of true community, and can help society to rebuild its hierarchy of human values and priorities. But awareness of the transcendent is the essential starting-point.

*   *   *   *   *

We are prophets

The baptised share Christ's role as prophet. It means that Christians can never shed responsibility for proclaiming the Good News of Jesus Christ, in season and out of season, to those who hear and heed the Word and to those who reject it, perhaps even with anger. It means as well that Christians have to interpret sensitively all human experience in the light of the Gospel so that through them ordinary men and women can discover for themselves its deeper significance. And it means, finally, holding up to society the mirror of truth so that it can see its real features in the light of the Gospel. In that sense, it purifies and reveals at one and the same time.

If we believe that Jesus Christ is the truth and the light, then the teaching role of his followers involves bringing to the whole of society the truth that sets

men free. The value, then, of the Christian's contribution to society by teaching, proclaiming and witnessing
to the truth is again of immense importance. Community depends on communication, and communication of
its nature has to be truthful. Community and society
wither when falsehood flourishes. Truth is indivisible
and it leads to God. The Christian – as witness to truth,
as defender of every genuine human value – can and
should exercise a salutary influence in the field of
education and in the public life of any nation.

The wealth of wisdom and experience contained in
divine revelation and in the tradition of the Church is at
the service of mankind. This ministry of truth is so
often brushed aside by society. Yet individuals and communities need to have a proper understanding of human
nature and its destiny. The modern world, and our
continent as a whole, can draw light and inspiration
from the current emphasis in Pope John Paul's teaching
on the dignity of man. It is a theme which runs through
the encyclicals of his pontificate. The Pope's preoccupa-
tion with the human person and his dignity would seem
to be rooted in his experiences in Poland when Communism and Christianity expressed fundamentally
opposed views on the human person and yet found in
man common ground for discussion and discovery.
Precisely here, in profound reflection on man, the
Christian can make a special contribution to society. As
Pope John Paul himself once said:

> "Perhaps one of the most obvious weaknesses of present-
> day civilisation lies in an inadequate view of man ... It
> is the drama of man being deprived of an essential dimen-
> sion of his being, namely the search for the infinite, and
> thus faced with having his very being reduced in the worst
> way" (Puebla, 28 January 1979).

The Christian makes the most effective contribution
by humbly initiating dialogue with others, dialogue
within the Church, dialogue with other religions, dialogue with those who do not believe in God, dialogue

with the secular world. The aim is always the discovery of truth and, in particular, the truth about man, and, having discovered it, to yield to the demands that it will always make.

* * * * *

We are kings

Our Lord was nailed to his Cross with the words over his head: "Jesus the Nazarene, King of the Jews". Was this recognition or ridicule by Pilate? It was certainly one of the charges levelled against him at his trial. And St John describes for us how the Roman soldiers mocked him by crowning him with thorns, dressing him in a purple robe and hailing him as king. At the height of his popularity, the accusation would not have seemed so extraordinary. After he had fed the five thousand by the lakeside, he had to flee to the hills when the crowds came to make him king. Much later Jesus had tried to explain to Pilate during his trial that he was indeed a king but that "mine is not a kingdom of this world". Earlier, as St Luke tells us, he had taught the pharisees: "The kingdom of God comes unwatched by men's eyes; there will be no saying, See it is here, or See, it is there; the kingdom of God is here, within you" (Lk 17,21).

We have to reflect very carefully about what the gospels tell us of the kingdom of God and Christ's own kingship. If through our Baptism we share that kingship, we should try to be clear what that means.

The kingdom of God is obviously something quite different from the secular State. It has nothing to do with power, domination and coercion. It is not based on race or tribe or self-interest. It is not concerned with rank or human estimates of worth and honour. It does not aim at securing the material prosperity and security of its citizens. It is clearly not subject to the limitations imposed by geography and time.

First and foremost the kingdom of God is an interior reality. Jesus himself said that those who are on the side of truth listen to his voice and belong to his kingdom (Jn 18,37). Its citizens are those who have died and are reborn through Baptism and faith in Jesus Christ. When they share his kingship, they are not changed outwardly, enjoy no material privileges or rewards; they are given something immeasurably greater and more lasting, an inner freedom from slavery to sin and from the power of death. They enter the kingdom but, in another sense, the kingdom enters them and transforms their inner selves, their minds and hearts, and in consequence begins to fashion new relationships with others. They live, as it were, in a different dimension, not subject to worldly assessment. The greatest among them may be the most despised and rejected in the kingdom of man. Like their master and king, they may themselves rule only from the Cross.

Those who share Christ's kingship will be concerned above all with the truth inside themselves, with carrying out the will of the Father, with walking the paths of righteousness. They will not seek success in the eyes of men. There is another scale of values for the followers of Christ the King. Who was the true victor on Calvary? Pilate? Those who refused to listen to Christ? Those who condemned and executed him? Or the innocent victim, seemingly defeated, who was to rise triumphant from the dead? In a cruel and unjust State, who is the truly free, the ultimate victor? The dictator, the torturer, the gaoler? Or the oppressed and the imprisoned, who retain integrity, ideals and faith?

There is great nobility to be found in those persons who have been called and have accepted to share in the passion of Jesus Christ, and perhaps throughout the whole of their lives. Theirs is a special vocation, and one generally not of their own choosing. The oppressed and persecuted are such, and so are the sick and the infirm, the handicapped and the sorrowful. They rule over their pain and sorrow, serene and free, among the privileged members of the kingdom of God.

It is a Christian instinct to accept from the hand of God the ills that befall us as well as the good. But we know that if life is harsh now, it will not be so when life is over. That is an important truth. But there is more to be said.

The kingdom of God is also an external reality. It is a kingdom of justice, truth, freedom and love, which the Church seeks to bring to birth in our divided and sinful world. There are moral laws to be upheld, human rights to be defended, Gospel values to be forwarded. This important task of the Church, with the problems and misunderstandings to which it may give rise, has been discussed in this book in the section entitled 'Building the kingdom of God'.

*   *   *

To understand and speak about the kingdom of God it is necessary to keep four aspects of that kingdom in mind. The kingdom of God is present now; it is at the same time a future reality. It is internal to the hearts and minds of the baptised; it is at the same time an external reality in the world. To emphasise one aspect and to neglect the others is to present an incomplete picture of the kingdom and can lead us badly astray; it can give a distorted view of the role of the Church in the world.

Notes on some Pilgrims and their tasks

The people of God on pilgrimage is made up of an endless variety of types. Each carries a special burden of responsibility – bishops, priests, religious and the laity who seek to sanctify the everyday world in which they live and work. There are the pilgrims who are marked out by the particular cross they carry, by the way they share the mystery of Christ's suffering. They are the handicapped, the dying, those asked by God to share the special pain of loneliness, especially those deserted by husbands or wives and called upon to raise a family on their own or to suffer the death of a marriage partner. There is here room for another book, another set of notes. In the following few pages I have recalled just some of the special groups to which I have addressed myself in recent years, but every group in the Church needs to feel the strength of Christ's presence, the encouragement of his teaching.

* * * * *

The family

The family is the universal school of life and the school of love. If the family is weakened, then the whole quality of life within our society is impaired, and the individual finds it even more difficult to learn how to love and to form mature and satisfactory relationships.

The Church, then, cannot concentrate simply on Christian marriage but on the situation of family life in today's society.

How do we as Catholic Christians view marriage? If we turn to the gospels to discover what Jesus Christ taught about marriage and the family, we might well be surprised at first to find out how little he said about it. Obviously he accepted and blessed marriage. His first miracle, the first sign he gave to the world in his ministry, took place while he was a guest at a wedding feast in Cana. More than once he emphasised the traditional precept of honouring father and mother. He taught his followers that married love was so precious that they should be on their guard against anything that might endanger it, against thoughts and longings as well as against more open betrayals.

The family is natural and basic. It responds to the need we have for each other. At the heart of the family is the love between husband and wife, a love which is natural and basic and which needs to be permanent. Although there is in the Church a Sacrament of marriage, religion did not invent marriage. It is not the preserve of Jew or Christian; it is the heritage of all humanity.

It is clear that the most important and characteristic feature of Christ's teaching on marriage was his insistence on its permanence, on the life-long commitment of husband and wife to each other. "What God has united, man must not divide". He was not formulating a set of precepts to impose on married people; instead he focussed on what he saw as the given reality. He saw what human love is and can be, and teaches how marriage can best express that love and prevent it from being spoiled or abused.

So the Christian view of marriage is about people, not just about believers; it is about people generally, people who love each other and come together to form a family; not just about a Christian family, but about any family. So the Christian teaching which rejects divorce is not meant simply as moral advice for believers. It is instead the necessary basis for human happiness and fulfilment in society. The Christian view of marriage as a life-long commitment of love between husband and wife in fact articulates the deepest, most genuine instincts of people in love. It is a profoundly moving experience. Their union, like that of their parents, like the overflowing goodness of God, is meant to be of its nature creative and fruitful. So, primarily because of their relationship to each other and because of the family to which they give birth, it is fundamental to the Christian view of marriage that the bond should be unbreakable.

Divorce then, which legally brings marriage to an end, is incompatible with this Christian view of marriage. We cannot compromise on this issue, though sometimes separation is inevitable. Sometimes it is possible to determine that the conditions necessary for a true union never existed from the outset of the marriage. In those cases a declaration of nullity can be given. But these are exceptional cases and not the rule. How do we help people accept the consequences of this teaching?

It is a pity that most pastoral and professional attention is directed towards marriages in crisis. If we are concerned exclusively with the care of the sick, we may ignore the needs of the healthy and that is the quickest way to swell the ranks of the sick. Most marriages last and are happy, but all marriages could be better. This is too important to be left to chance. We cannot simply celebrate a wedding service and then leave couples to their own resources. We need to support and sustain families at every stage of their development, but especially in the early years. When stress nevertheless develops, and breakdown occurs, the Church recognises and claims its proper role, namely that of healing without reproach. It is important always to be firm on principle, but compassionate towards individuals.

Pope John Paul spoke at York on the subject of marriage: "Treasure your families. Protect their rights. Support the family by your laws and administration. Allow the voice of the family to be heard in the making of your policies. The future of your society, the future of humanity, passes by way of the family".

*   *   *   *   *

Ideal of motherhood

Wives and mothers, bearing the brunt of domestic chores day by day in their homes, should never forget the importance of their service there. It was not for nothing that Our Lord spent thirty years of his life at home doing ordinary things, and only spent some two or three years preaching the Gospel. Ordinary things have an extraordinary value in the eyes of God, especially when done as acts of love, love of God and love of the family. But their special value comes from the fact that God became man, lived a family life in Nazareth with Mary and Joseph, and thereby sanctified the ordinary and gave it meaning.

Catholic mothers know, but may forget from time to time, that they can become saints in the home. Similarly, of course, the daily round in the office, in the factory, at home, can lead to holiness, because holiness consists in doing ordinary things extraordinarily well. No way of life, no set of responsibilities excludes people from sanctity, nor dispenses them from striving for it. Every act, however small and unimportant, can be an act of love. One day, if we have remained faithful to our vocation, we shall hear God say: "Well done, good and faithful servant", because we have been faithful over little things.

Family life is not made up of time spent in the kitchen, or round the table or in domestic work. It is people who matter, and what greater vocation can there be than to bring up a family. Catholic mothers do not need me to tell them that, but it is good for all of us to be reminded of it. Our Lord, as man, had to learn, and who did he learn from at the beginning? Who gave him the example which every child needs? Who gave him the affection and tenderness that enables the growing child to become the mature adult? It was his mother.

Mothers have their worries, their disappointments, their heartbreaks. Mary too was sometimes puzzled and in distress. She had to flee with her son into Egypt; once she lost him on a pilgrimage. She saw him dying and in agony. It is sometimes like that for mothers. When it happens, it is hard to make sense of it. You have to trust and go on trusting. A sword pierced Our Lady's heart; it will sometimes pierce yours. She was perhaps closest to him when she had to share most intimately in his passion. So it will be with you.

When hard times come your way and you are asked to share in the passion of Christ, then you will know you are very close to Our Lord and to his mother. In every pain and sorrow there are deep joys and peace to be discovered. This is the happiness of being one with him.

*   *   *   *   *

Work

Since so much of our life is devoted to work it is important for us to understand that all human work is sanctified and sanctifying. It is sanctified because the Lord himself devoted much of his life to it. It is sanctifying because everything that is good contributes to giving honour and glory to God. Work is never a penalty for sin. It belongs to the nature of man. So, whether I work at an office desk, in the home, on the land or in a factory, my work is an act of love. So, in daily life, we do not witness to Jesus only when we speak about him but our work itself is a prayer. That is one reason why unemployment so grieves the Church and so invites its concern. Work is part of our humanity. Deprived of it, we feel ourselves threatened and devalued.

If we are seriously trying to live according to the mind of Christ, we will obviously want to throw ourselves wholeheartedly and with all our skills into our work. We will never be content merely to watch the clock and to regard employment simply as a means to pay the bills and have a good time. There will be legitimate pride in what we do. We will want to master our craft or our profession so as to give greater glory to God.

It can be painful and soul-destroying to be faced with redundancy, early retirement or long periods of unemployment. It is too early yet to know whether the present industrial troubles of our country are temporary or long-term. Certainly many are faced with the necessity of making sense out of enforced idleness. Perhaps we are entering a period of history when our advanced technology will make full employment a thing of the past, perhaps we will need to change our ideas. Should we continue to think that work always equals paid employment? How can we hold on to the sense of our own value if we are not earning a wage or salary? What can we do to make use of our enforced inactivity? It would be unbearable for outsiders to suggest to those currently unemployed how best to profit by that experience. The answers must come from within the situation and from those who are so seriously disadvantaged.

Those who are at work should try to grasp the significance of what they do. It is easier of course if our work is involved with agriculture and horticulture, with growing things. It becomes more obvious that we labour alongside God the Creator. Tilling the land, irrigating the soil and gathering the harvest are profoundly and traditionally part of being human. The sweat of our brow and the physical exhaustion of heavy manual work may be the result of sin and our fallen state. But work is not itself a curse but a blessing. It befits human dignity: it confers dignity. It is noble and ennobling.

That is because work is a sharing in the creative act of God. Creation was not a single event many million years ago. It is a present fact. Through work we labour with the energy and power God has given us, and so surely with His purposes in our minds.

The land has its own secrets, its own laws. Those laws have been determined by a mind that is above and beyond us – if I may use a very human way of expressing it. The secrets, slowly discovered by us, are known to the Creator. Our discoveries are explorations of His mind. Those who are close to nature are more likely to be humble before it. We have begun to realise that our environment and its natural resources are not inert, inexhaustible. We are not at liberty merely to exploit planet Earth by means of our technology. Not only must we conserve our limited inheritance but we should learn its inner nature. We should attempt to work with natural forces and not abuse or pollute the earth. Humankind is but slowly attuning itself to the rhythms and laws of nature.

It is, I fully realise, more difficult to achieve a religious perspective on other kinds of work. It is certainly possible if our job brings us into contact with other people, and especially if we are engaged in healing, serving, counselling or educating them. It is obvious then that we are making a positive contribution to the good of others. It is not too difficult to try to see the face of Christ in those we encounter. Our work for others can readily be transformed into service of him.

The vast majority of working people are not so fortunate. For them, work is much more impersonal; it is repetitive, boring, undemanding. Most people who work in factories and offices are remote from the public; they rarely see the finished product or share the satisfaction of exercising initiative and imagination.

It requires of them a huge leap of faith to see their work as part of God's continuing creation.

Understandably the coal-face or the steel rolling-mill is no place to stand back and reflect on the meaning of work. Mind and heart are not easily lifted to God in the noise and the sweat of intensely physical work. There may be snatched moments of vocal prayer. By and large, however, it is a matter of developing an attitude during times of leisure and silence, so that we have an approach to work, and an understanding of it, that will sustain us throughout our day.

Even the most repetitive task, even the most exhausting labour, can be lifted up to God, made holy. Without work of this kind, our economy would not function, and our cities and towns would not operate. We would not be housed, clothed, warmed, fed. Our national prosperity would decline; our people be plunged into hardship. All work is for the people; all of it keeps life going. In that sense, work is part of God's continuing creation. We must see it as a whole, and not be put off because the part we play seems relatively unimportant.

Cardinal Cardijn, that great apostle of the workers, used to say: "No work – no Mass". It was his way of getting working people to see that their efforts made life possible and helped to shape the offering we make at each Mass. Builders construct the church; quarrymen bring the stone for the altar; miners dig the coal which fuels power-stations for heat and light; weavers make the linen for the vestments and the altar-cloths; farmers produce the wheat for the bread and the grapes for the wine; public transport workers and the car-plant men make it possible for the congregation to gather. All in their own way, through their work, make the Mass possible. We bring ourselves, our work, all that we have, to the Mass. We offer bread and wine – 'the work of human hands' – and we offer it with Christ our brother. The Father accepts our offering, and Christ is made present to us and for us in the form of our gifts, the bread and wine made by our labour. God's daily miracle could not take place without human work. No work, no Mass. It is important to make that connection.

Work, even in the most unfavourable circumstances, can still offer opportunities for individuals to grow and find themselves. Almost no work is solitary. Modern industry, though in some respects it may seem totally dehumanizing, allows men and women at work to find friendship, laughter and human solidarity. It is important for any worker to remain aware of this aspect of work and to support and encourage others in every possible way. A smile, a cheery word, an unobtrusive good-turn can work wonders.

Despite everything, the human spirit cannot be quenched and human dignity is ultimately re-asserted. It is important for the committed follower of Christ the worker to be on the alert to assert human rights and defend human dignity in the work-place. Some will find it possible to take an active part in the work of trade unions, some will be content simply to maintain their own integrity and self-respect, but that too can encourage and sustain others.

While there is work, there is hope. The work of individuals contributes to that hope by supporting life and developing prosperity. As a sharing in God's continuing creation it helps us look expectantly to the future. Whenever we pray, we can lift up to God hands that are never empty.

*   *   *   *   *

The Pope and ministry

One of the most moving moments at the election of a Pope is when the man who has been elected goes out of the Sistine Chapel dressed as a cardinal in order to change into the papal robes. At that moment he appears

like a sad and seemingly broken man, weighed down by
the burden of what has been put on his shoulders. He
goes out of a door at the side, and a few moments
later he comes back, all in white. He is the Pope, and he
is transformed. He comes back looking quite different,
almost new. In a sense the cardinals who have elected
him are now different; our attitude to that particular
man changes. He went out of the room one of us; he
came back as our Pope, the Vicar of Christ, our leader.

Then each of us goes up to him to kiss his ring and
promise him obedience. We then line up and go in procession from the Sistine Chapel to the balcony where he
is to bless for the first time that large crowd of persons
gathered below in the Square of St Peter. We process,
the young cardinals first and the older ones at the back,
and behind us all the Pope. Suddenly the sight of open
windows becomes too tempting. We break ranks and
rush to see this vast crowd of people stretching as far as
the eye can see. Then the explosion of excitement and
cheering, as people catch sight of the Pope for the first
time.

What struck me at that moment was the thought of
the parable of the shepherd who left his ninety-nine
sheep to go in search of the hundredth one which had
been lost. It was that parable the other way round. Now
the sheep were clamouring for their shepherd. Here he
was, called to provide leadership for seven hundred million Catholics, and for all those millions of other Christians and non-Christians who today look to the Holy
Father for leadership in the things of God.

These moments are precious memories. They also are
like signposts pointing to things that really matter. It
is my firm belief that people today are hungry. They
may not know what they are hungry for, but they are
hungry: hungry for truth about life as a whole, and
hungry for truth about their own lives and the meaning
of them. They want to be told things that will give them
strength, comfort and a sense of direction. They need to
know what will make life worth living.

We may have our moments of doubt and confusion,

yet on the whole our faith sustains and guides us. Imagine the darkness, the loneliness and the emptiness of being totally without faith of any kind. People try to supply themselves with all kinds of things which in fact do not enlighten, sustain or fulfil them. Modern man is left unsatisfied and restless.

These thoughts are relevant to the question of vocations. Every Christian has, especially today, a vocation to be a missioner, to carry the message of Christ into every situation of life and work. That is a responsibility given to all of us through our Baptism and Confirmation. In addition, we sorely need men and women prepared to dedicate themselves full-time either to the priesthood or to the religious life, in order to give that witness and service which is special to priests and religious. The need is great. The number of full-time ministers has dwindled, and those in the field are on average older than in the past. The harvest is riper than we know, and we need labourers for the reaping.

We have to pray, in season and out, every day, that young men and young girls will come forward and present themselves for work as priests or religious. There is room for different temperaments and for different levels of ability. We need men and women with powers of leadership, and with generosity, who would in all circumstances make a considerable contribution to society. There is room for all, yet we particularly need gifted people. Our prayers will be necessary if they are to make a generous response, because it is my experience that young men and women of talent sense that they need to make a greater sacrifice. The lure of worldly success, the attraction of going far in life is strong. It needs courage and far-sightedness to resist it and put oneself at the service of the Church. That is the kind of sacrifice being asked of young Catholics in the West. It is not a matter of danger, of physical hardship. We belong to a Church that has not suffered in recent times as the Church in Eastern Europe and in the Third World often has. We have become a slightly spoiled and pampered Church compared with many others. Yet it is still possible for us to create a spirituality and asceticism of the Cross without the pressure of external persecution or hardship. We have to see through the allure of consumerism and materialism and gear ourselves for the pressures of pilgrimage.

*   *   *   *   *

The priesthood

Jesus Christ is the priest, the teacher and the shepherd. To have said that is already to have indicated clearly what are the priorities for every bishop and for every priest.

As priests, our first task and responsibility is to stand day by day at the altar to enable our parish communities to share in that greatest of all events which is the Sacrifice of the Mass. We remember that this great act of worship cannot come to pass without the priest. The role of the priest is fundamental and essential. We are never, in a sense, more truly ourselves than when we stand at the altar presiding over the eucharistic celebration of our communities.

As teachers, our task is to portray and expound the Word of God. Our proclamation has to live. It is communicated to others in proportion as we have made it our own. From our lips should be heard not only that Word of God which we find in the Scriptures, but a word from God out of a heart that is full with the experience of God within us.

As shepherds, our task is to care for those committed to our charge, helping wounded humanity on its pilgrimage through the complexities and difficulties of modern life. We must guide the people of God to take its responsibility to bring the Gospel to a secular world that does not know and does not recognise God. The healing hand which we can extend to those who are as weak and frail as we are, is Christ's loving hand. The words we pronounce, the gestures we make, are his words, his gestures transmitted through us.

The only priesthood is that of Christ, and it is entrusted into our hands. The people of God should see in us an icon, or image, of Christ the high priest. Our hands handle his sacred realities, our lips proclaim his holy Word and explain it. Whatever the circumstances of the Church at any moment in history, can we ever doubt the dignity which is ours by Ordination? Can we ever belittle the heavy responsibility that has been laid upon our shoulders?

We carry a burden, but we recognise that the burden of Christ is sweet and his yoke light. He gives the help we need, so there is never any reason for us to fear, to draw back or to be discouraged. Christ enables us all the time to respond to his call, as fresh and vivid today and as compelling, as it was on the day of our Ordination.

Have I the heart of a priest? Is my heart in my priesthood? Or has my treasure become something other than my priesthood? Do I sense still a certain thrill as I go to the altar to celebrate Mass, or is it a bit different now? Do I long to speak to the people of the good news of the Gospel, or has it become dull and uninteresting for me, and so uninteresting when I speak about it? Do I love the sick and the poor? Does my priestly heart still feel for those in distress? Do I feel awe and reverence for the Blessed Sacrament, or has familiarity – or, worse still, doubt – coloured my attitude? Do I still feel a terrible humility and awesome responsibility as I say in the confessional: "I absolve you from your sins . . ."?

Forgive me, Lord, for my failures and shortcomings, but I know deep down that you use me as you found me, and in spite of myself. That is consoling, but give me, I pray, the heart of a priest, especially a heart that knows the meaning of true love, love of God and love of the people. May I be helped to translate that love into action and into service of others.

* * * * *

Priestly jubilees

No priest will ever be able to understand to the full the significance of the power that has been given to him at Ordination. Fifty years later a priest should be celebrating Mass each day with ever deeper reverence and attention. His faithfulness and his daily meditation should have uncovered for him treasures of understanding that he could not have dreamed of as a young priest. Can there be a greater privilege than to celebrate Mass for half a century?

What greater task is there for the priest than to sit in the confessional week by week and say to troubled and tortured souls, "I absolve you in the name of the Father, the Son and the Holy Spirit"? What could equal the deep satisfaction of consoling the sick and the dying, and strengthening them with the Sacrament of the sick?

These are great acts but we often cannot see clearly the effects of what we do. That is why a priest has to be a man of faith. He can only be a man of faith if he is a man of prayer. It is prayer which keeps faith alive, and it is through faith that the priest deepens his appreciation of the mystery of God which is the sacramental system.

No priest, looking back, can feel complete satisfaction, because he recognises the greatness and dignity of what he has been asked to do. As he gets older, he becomes more aware of his frailty. There is perhaps a grace that recognises weakness and deficiency in ourselves as well as in others.

Fidelity, one of the loveliest qualities in any person, is an essential quality in the following of Jesus Christ. It makes us stay with him when the going is rough and when the way is not always clear. It helps us to respond to him when he calls: "Follow me". Just as we need faith to recognise and appreciate the great dignity of the priesthood, so we need to trust to stay with Our Lord. It is that faith, that trust which is hope, which inspires priests throughout their lives to love and serve the people.

*   *   *   *   *

Vocations

The Church has a responsibility to foster vocations, to encourage men and women to enter into religious life, and to urge men to consider the possibility of a call to the priesthood.

That responsibility to foster vocations has to be exercised in the first place by two sets of persons – parents and school teachers. They have the first responsibility to put before young people the idea that perhaps God is calling them either to religious life, or to a life as a diocesan priest.

There is so much to say about the priesthood and the call to the religious life. I never cease to be amazed and delighted by that most surprising of all vocations, the call of Levi who became Matthew. He was a tax-collector, a man who by profession was not observing the strict laws of his people and of his religion. He was a renegade and a greedy one. Everything was against him. Yet Our

Lord called him, showing the total freedom God has. He does not call because He finds virtue; He calls and forms virtue in those He chooses. It was a most remarkable choice, underlining the truth of St John's words: "You did not choose me, I chose you".

So a vocation is always a question of God's choice. But somehow or other it is possible in practice to miss hearing that call. Many people I have known have dismissed from their minds the possibility of a vocation. "It is not for me; I'm not good enough", or "There is no example of a vocation in my family". A hundred and one reasons are given why people should close their minds to the possibility that God might be calling them.

A priest in his Ordination service is described as a co-worker of the bishop. A bishop at his own Ordination is called to be a teacher and shepherd. To be a priest in the strict sense is to be somebody involved in the sacramental life of the Church. A bishop has to be a prophet, priest and shepherd, a successor of the Apostles, responsible to God for the faithful of his diocese, and with a further responsibility for the welfare of the world-wide Church. Priests are part of the bishop's work since they represent him in the parishes and are his co-workers.

We have to communicate to young people the extra-ordinary thing to which they might be called; what it is to stand at the altar and hold in their hands the Body and Blood of Our Lord. When the priest says: "This is my body, this is my blood", he is talking of a relation-ship with Christ which is quite special.

There is profound significance still to be fully un-covered in the role of the priest as minister of the sacra-ments, as the channel of divine life. When the Holy Father was in this country, he came as a pastor adminis-tering the sacraments. In this way he underlined their importance in the life of the Church. The sacraments will be at the heart of renewal in the Church.

The Pope is successor of Peter. He, like Peter, con-firms the faith of his brethren. So, pre-eminently among the bishops, he is a teacher of the faith. When he came to Britain he spoke clearly on many issues, about family life, about peace, about ecumenism and Church unity. His words had great impact. Television, radio and the press carried them into every home. It was a remarkable and unparalleled experience of popular evangelisation. Where he led we must find a way to follow. Bishops and priests, we must speak the truth on such matters too, and find ways of getting it across forcefully to people.

Parents can talk about these things to their families, and school teachers to their pupils, and hold up to them the wonderful ideal of the priesthood. They can explain how necessary and essential the priesthood is to the work of God in the world. There has always been in our country a special relationship of affection and trust between priest and people. It was forged in times of shared danger and hardship. Parents and teachers by their attitudes to their bishop and priests help to hand down this fine tradition of love and respect for the priesthood. That in itself creates in young minds some questions about the role and the relevance of the priesthood and the possibility of a response.

*   *   *   *   *

Fostering vocations

Our Lord Jesus Christ said: "The harvest indeed is great, but the labourers are few. Pray, then, that the Father in heaven will send more labourers".

Many things are important in a vocation. First, it is a gift from God as a response to prayer. Very often it is the prayer of a person hidden away, perhaps living alone, suffering and lonely, but praying for priests and praying for religious.

The second important thing in fostering vocations is,

without any doubt at all, the quality of family life. There have to be parents who are dedicated to God, who give an example of good Christian living, who instinctively judge things in the light of the Gospel, who do not push or fuss but are sensible and cheerful in their service of God. To grow up in that kind of family is a preparation second to none for a boy or girl entering into a dedicated life. A good religious, if I may call on my own experience, receives his or her first novitiate in the family. The first lessons in prayer are not given in the seminary or novitiate; they are given in the home.

The third important factor is the school which plays a very important part. Its influence is not to be found so much in what happens during organised classes devoted to the teaching of religion, but rather in the dedication of teachers. If they are committed Christians, then they will communicate something of their interest in the things of God and their enthusiasm for the Gospel to those with whom they come in contact. Again, if I may call upon experience, I have known people enter religious life because of a chance remark made by a teacher in a certain circumstance or situation, and that teacher has never remembered making the remark; or it may have been the influence of someone who was not a particularly good teacher. Yet the young person has instinctively felt that here was someone who embodied in his or her life special values or significance.

Prayer, the family, and the school are the important influences which will continue to provide candidates for the seminaries, and novices for the religious orders. At the same time, we must be aware that the call of God comes to a Matthew or a Mary Magdalene – out of the blue, as it were, and against the odds.

* * * * *

Religious life

We live in a period of history today where, under God, religious orders have to show a new creativity, perhaps even originality. To read the signs of the times and respond to them is never easy; the task seems too great, and the problems too numerous.

Every religious engaged in active work should carry within her a disappointment that she is not enclosed in a life of constant, unremitting prayer. In every Sacred Heart nun there should be a disappointed Carmelite; just as in every Benedictine there should be a disappointed Carthusian.

Religious should never lose a certain nostalgia for the desert. If they have nostalgia for the desert, then they will be safe in the market place.

They must be loyal to their profession and recognise again the radical nature of it, and what it means to be vowed to obedience, poverty and a life of virginity. It is radical, and if lived to the full will sometimes hurt intensely. But it is always a source of deep happiness and the way for a religious to union with God.

*   *   *   *   *

The sick and the handicapped

Lourdes has an important lesson to teach us. The most important people there are the sick and the handicapped. They are given all the important places at Mass and in the processions. Everyone makes room for them to pass. We visit them in the hospitals and there pay our respects to them. The reason why we do this is because we know that Our Lord has a special love for the sick and the handicapped. And if that is so of Our Lord, it has to be so of ourselves as well.

The sick and the handicapped have a place in God's plan. We do not see or understand that plan. We are often baffled by the suffering that so many sick and handicapped must endure, and especially so when it occurs in our own family. We have to trust in God's great love and in His goodness, and never give up doing so.

Those who are sick or handicapped have then a special vocation in the Church. Sickness and disability borne with patience and courage in the name of Jesus Christ, are as noble as the suffering and death of a martyr accepted in defence of the faith. That daily patience and courage is, for many, more difficult than suffering and death accepted once and for all. A community that does not honour its old, sick and handicapped is incomplete; there is something missing. A lesson has not been learned.

To some extent we all limp along the road. Some of us are physically dependent on others and must be helped, but is there any one of us who does not carry a load, a secret sorrow, a gnawing anxiety, a hidden fear, or who is not burdened by guilt or overwhelmed by some pressure? All of us are therefore to a greater or lesser extent handicapped. Those who are sick or handicapped can by their lives preach to us who are perhaps not handicapped physically but in so many other ways.

The patience, courage, cheerfulness, spirituality of those who suffer often give more to us than we can give to them.

*   *   *

We can race vigorously and confidently towards God; we can leap from our stretcher like the paralytic healed by Christ in the gospel; but most of us move from death to life with stumbling steps. We falter on the road. We experience the stiffness and bruising of our past and of our failures. We encounter real pain and suffering. All of us experience moments of despair and distress. We may be sick or handicapped. We may realise that we are old and unloved. We may have been deserted or let down. We may be out of work and losing our pride.

At times of great distress and confusion, thinking may only add to the pain; praying will be impossible. The only helpful thing, the only possible thing, is to sit or kneel looking at the crucifix, the image of Christ dying on the Cross. We may indeed have to share the darkness which was in Christ when he prayed that psalm from the Cross: "My God, my God, why hast Thou forsaken me?" We can do no more than just look at the crucifix, but we can do no better, for then it will give up its secret. It will speak to us, in our misery, of hope and encouragement.

There is no tidy, rational explanation of the crushing burden of suffering. We cannot work out easy answers about why it should be. God gave us instead not an answer, but a way to find the answer. It is the Cross that will reveal it, but it has to be a personal discovery. You cannot begin to see pattern and purpose unless you have known the Cross and blindly let Jesus lead you from despair into hope.

* * *

No words can substitute for the actual experience of being close to those who are handicapped or suffering. Once, when visiting a hospital for the mentally handicapped, I was particularly struck when I went into a small ward of adolescents. They had been born blind, deaf, and mentally handicapped.

It takes an act of faith to be able to say, as St Thomas More said, "Nothing can come but that which is God's will, and that indeed will be best".

As I left that little ward, I could only reflect that one day I will see them again and that they will be the privileged among the loved ones of God. He sees in them a beauty which we cannot see. He has a plan for them which we cannot understand. Those born blind will one day open their eyes and, to their delight, the first thing they see will be the vision of the All-beautiful, God.

* * * * *

The challenge to young people

"You are, my dear friends, the Church of today and the hope of tomorrow." Do you remember those words of the Holy Father at Ninian Park, and do you remember how they were cheered and clapped, clapped and cheered? I thought then, what will happen when the cheering and clapping stop? Some months later on, will the young remember and what will they do about it? Would today's enthusiasm in Ninian Park become tomorrow's forgotten ideal? That is always the problem when you have an occasion like a papal visit or a Holy Year. We whip ourselves up, and then we are in danger of sliding back into our previous apathy.

We should remind ourselves of another phrase of the Holy Father's: "This is the greatest contribution you can make in your lives, to communicate Christ to the world". How are we going to do that? How can any of us do that unless we have first learnt about Christ, who he is, what he is and what he demands, what he asks and what he commands. When the Holy Father picked out, from all the activities in which we can engage, the means of learning about Christ, he picked out prayer and said: "That is the way you do it, because if you learn about Christ in prayer you then get a sense of mission". Once we start praying, once we start discovering about Christ, then we want to talk to other people about him;

we want to spread the Good News. It is natural to want
to do so; we gain a sense of mission.

The Holy Father went on to say that if we pray, if
we learn about Our Lord, we will be able to read the
signs of the times, namely, what God seems to be asking
of us in our day, in our society. There are two which
come to mind. They are perhaps of all the things the
Holy Father said when he was with us the two he most
emphasised: Christian unity and peace. We should not
forget what he said about Christian unity; he said we
each have a responsibility to work for it. Again, in every
homily, in every address, he spoke about the importance
of building peace; peace in our hearts, peace in our
families, peace in our neighbourhood, peace in our
country, peace between nations.

People are often daunted by challenges as big as
Christian unity and peace. There is only one way to
respond – gradually. Individuals have to start creating
Christian unity in their own neighbourhood, among
their own friends, wherever they are. Similarly, they
have to begin working for peace wherever they are: in
their places of work, their homes, their own national
groupings. It is easy to be committed to the universal
ideal, and then to neglect the demands of the particular and local situation. We start from where we are.

The Pilgrim's End

The evening of life
The hour of our death
After death
The moment of ecstasy

The evening of life

"The wind dropped and there was deep calm". Our Lord and his apostles were in the boat together and a great storm of wind arose and drove the waves into the boat. Jesus was in the stern of that boat, asleep, and his apostles aroused him saying: "Master, art thou unconcerned? We are sinking". So he rose up, checked the wind and said to the sea: "Peace, be still", and the wind dropped and there was deep calm. Then he said to them: "Why are you faint-hearted, have you still no faith?" But they were overcome with awe.

It is like that in our lives. We leave the harbour where the sea is calm, as we grow from childhood into the adult world, and then we must begin to battle against the storms of everyday life, its problems and its conflicts. Then, surely, as the evening of our life approaches, we enter once again into peaceful waters, when the wind has dropped and there is deep calm. In the middle years – the high noon of life – the Lord may often seem to be asleep, or at any rate we think him unconcerned, uninterested. But of course there is another explanation. There is so much to do, so much to face that we have become too absorbed in our own activity and not sufficiently concerned about him. The hustle and bustle of life can squeeze him out of our thoughts and very far from our desires.

Words like 'hope', 'expectation' and 'looking forward' have, wrongly in my view, been stolen by the young from the old. Those are the words proper to the elderly, because by the very nature of things they now look forward to the vision of God. That vision is the fulfilment of all that they have ever wanted; they look forward to enjoying that ecstasy of love which is union with God. If such fulfilment does not come at the end of a life well spent, then the toils of life have been in vain. Such frustration is impossible to imagine. The joy and peace which we have known from time to time in a fitful fashion will be ours totally and for all time. We were made for that and that alone.

The senior citizens have, in God's providence, a kind of priority. They are in the outer chamber waiting for the final entry into the kingdom. That should be a cause of peace, a cause of joy; one day forward, one step nearer.

Is this too rosy a picture of what life is like, or should be like? After all, our energy and our strength today is not what it was yesterday. There are problems and there are aches and pains which we did not know in the afternoon of our lives. At such times, it is only by looking at Christ crucified on the Cross that we can ever make sense of what befalls us. When asked to share those sufferings we should accept it as a gift. All pain is mysteriously also gift from God because pain can purify and prepare us for the vision of Him whose love is stronger than the strongest love of a woman for her child, or a lover for the beloved.

A well-ordered society honours and respects its senior citizens, cares for their needs, ensures their well-being. The old have a gift beyond compare. They have had the opportunity to learn wisdom in the school of life. Wisdom must be prized above skill, cleverness or expertise. In the Bible, in more settled times, the old were valued by the mature and by the young. We need to remember that.

* * * * *

The hour of our death

We live in a rapidly changing world. Nothing is certain. One thing is: we all face death.

It is a sombre thought. We find all sorts of ways of forgetting about it. We use expressions which empty it of finality and threat. We talk about "going to the other side" or "passing away". Yet it is the Christian instinct to be brave and to face the meaning of death fairly and squarely. We face it because it is inescapable, one of life's harsh realities. Whenever a member of the family, or a colleague, dies we are reminded very vividly that it is the one thing which will happen to each one of us. Dying can be a very lonesome experience, for nothing can be more isolating than pain.

One day I shall die. Thinking about that is good for me. It helps me to look at the way I am living. It enables me to get a better perspective. I know that I shall not remain forever in this world. I must ask important questions: "Am I making the best of my life? Am I living in such a way that I try always to follow my conscience? Are my motives in life right? What do I really want? What am I really seeking?" Those are very simple and fundamental questions, and ones that we have to ask ourselves.

That is a sobering thought. While such thoughts have their value, it would be quite wrong to leave it like that. The Christian faces death realistically, but also knows that death is a gateway, a new beginning, a fulfilment of human life.

I fail to understand how anybody can go through life and think there is nothing after death. That is a totally inhuman thought. Now life for the majority is not easy. There are periods of joy and happiness of course; there are times when things go smoothly and happily; yet there are a great number of times when it is a burden. Life is punctuated now with joys, now with sorrows. Within us is the desire to live; we want to go on. There is an urge to go on living fully and totally.

We long to enjoy deep down the peace, the joy and happiness which constantly elude us. We cannot grasp them now nor keep them.

It is for that deep joy and happiness that we were made. One day it will be ours. If it were not going to be ours our lives would certainly end in frustration and be unfulfilled. That is not only a terrible thing to contemplate, but it is to my way of thinking unreasonable.

We are men and women moving through life like pilgrims heading towards our final destination. It is healthy to look forward to that destination when we shall find total fulfilment. That fulfilment must consist in an experience of love because love is the highest of all human experience. To love totally, to be loved completely. It is in union with that which is most lovable that we become fully ourselves.

Do not be fearful of death. Welcome it when it comes. It is now a holy thing, made so by him who died that we might live.

*   *   *   *   *

After death

A priest started his homily at a funeral saying: "I am going to preach about 'judgment' ". There was dismay in the congregation. Then he went on: "Judgment is whispering into the ear of a merciful and compassionate God the story of my life which I had never been able to tell".

Many of us have a story, or part of one at any rate, about which we have never been able to speak to anyone. Fear of being misunderstood, inability to understand ourselves, ignorance of the darker side of our hidden lives, or just shame, make it very difficult for many people. Our true story is not told, or only half of it is. What a relief it will be to be able to whisper freely and fully into that merciful and compassionate ear. After all that is what He has always wanted. He waits for us to come home to Him. He receives us, His prodigal children, now contrite and humble with an embrace. In that embrace we start to tell Him our story, and He begins that process of healing and preparation which we call Purgatory.

* * *

The apostles Peter, James and John, had been fishing all night, and they had caught nothing. Our Lord told them to let down their nets, and this they did. The catch was good. "When Simon Peter saw him, he fell at the knees of Jesus, saying, 'Leave me, Lord; I am a sinful man'" (Lk 5,8).

Peter did not want to be parted from Jesus. That is why he clung to his knees. At the same time he recognised his unworthiness. He felt he could not remain in Our Lord's presence. He wanted to be close, yet he felt he should keep away. He was not worthy.

This is perhaps the way it will be for us after death. We have lived and worked, sometimes succeeding, sometimes failing. He has waited for us. We are in His presence. We whisper our story into His compassionate ear. We know that He understands. But we are not yet ready for the vision of Him. We are in need of healing, of being purified. We shall not want to see Him until we are prepared for it. We shall go happily to Purgatory, certain that it is for a time only. He will wait for us.

* * *

It is possible to refuse to go to Him. It is possible to deny Him, to adore not Him but false gods, to hate Him even. We can walk away deliberately. We can choose self, self alone, above and before all. We shall live on, lonely, barren, empty, miserable lives. That is hell.

* * * * *

The moment of ecstasy

This life is a period of training, a time of preparation, during which we learn the art of loving God and our neighbour, the heart of the Gospel message, sometimes succeeding, sometimes failing.

Death is the way which leads us to the vision of God, the moment when we shall see Him as He really is, and find our total fulfilment in love's final choice.

The ultimate union with that which is most lovable, union with God, is the moment of ecstasy, the unending 'now' of complete happiness. That vision will draw from us the response of surprise, wonder and joy which will be forever our prayer of praise. We are made for that.

*The Society of St Paul and
the Daughters of St Paul
at the service of the Church*

> I became the servant of the Church when God made me responsible for delivering God's message to you, the message which was a mystery hidden for generations and centuries and now has been revealed to his saints.
>
> *St Paul to the Church at Colossae*

Since the days when Christ walked among the stones in the desert places of Palestine, the mind of man has devised wonders for the people of the world. Machinery has changed the nature of labour, great roads speed our way to capital cities; in the twinkling of an eye computers calculate matters most intricate — above all, nations can communicate with one another by radio and television and film, by telephone and telex, by newspapers and magazines and books in every language.

How marvellous to be able to use the power of technology to spread to the entire world the healing message of Christ — to take his words, preached in a little country so long ago, to every corner of the Earth!

This was the dream of young James Alberione as he knelt in a lonely vigil of prayer, on New Year's Eve 1900. And from the inspiration of that vigil was to come, in 1914, the Society of St Paul, the religious congregation of priests and brothers who spread the christian message through the mass media. In 1915, he founded the Daughters of St Paul — sisters who would dedicate themselves to the same apostolate.

From their early days both the Society of St Paul and the Daughters of St Paul have poured effort and imagination into making their Founder's dream a reality. Working side by side, they communicate the word of Christ as writers, broadcasters, film-makers, television producers, printers and photographers, publishers and journalists, shop-managers and sales-hands. Under Fr Alberione's vigorous leadership, until his death in 1971, the priests, brothers and sisters have taken root in thirty countries all over the world.

In Britain since 1947, the Society of St Paul prints and publishes books, produces and distributes audiovisual aids, under the imprint of St Paul Publications. The Daughters of St Paul offer their service to the Church through their small but distinctive chain of religious Book Centres.

The Church, at the Second Vatican Council, declared that "it is one of her duties to announce the Good News of Salvation also with the help of the media of social communication and to instruct men in their proper use". The Society of St Paul and the Daughters of St Paul have the Church's official mandate to promote the christian message through the mass media.

Characteristics of the two religious congregations as expressed in their Constitutions:

Our aim. Sent to proclaim to man the truth that makes him free, we assume in the Church the specific role she entrusts to us, the work of evangelisation with the media of social communication: press, films, radio, television, records — all the inventions which human progress furnishes and the needs and conditions of the times require.

Our religious witness. We dedicate our strength, our person and our time to this mission to which we are committed as community.

Religious consecration through the vows animates and sustains our apostolic activity and makes us completely available for the service of Truth.

Our target. Animated by the spirit of St Paul, we direct the message to all men without distinction of culture, class or boundary. Unable to reach all men at once, we seek to reach the masses, giving preference to the poor, to those furthest away from the faith.

Following the example of Christ, we proclaim the message of salvation with fidelity and integrity, adapting it to various mentalities and environmental situations, with due respect for the authentic values found in every culture and tradition.

And our future. Promoting the christian message through the mass media is nowadays of critical importance. Many adult christians still need help in becoming mature christians. Young people, the hope of the Church, cry out for religious experience, for authentic Christian life. Those in search of truth are to be offered the word of God. The Society of St Paul and the Daughters of St Paul have a major role in this programme. They have laid their foundations, but their work needs to develop and diversify — it needs people who are eager to share with others the wealth of their faith.